THE DIVINE RELATIVITY
A SOCIAL CONCEPTION OF GOD

THE
DIVINE RELATIVITY

A Social Conception of God

BY

CHARLES HARTSHORNE

NEW HAVEN AND LONDON

YALE UNIVERSITY PRESS

International standard book number: 0-300-00539-3
Printed in the United States of America by
The Colonial Press Inc.,
Clinton, Massachusetts.
Published in Great Britain, Europe, and Africa by
Yale University Press, Ltd., London.
Distributed in Latin America by Kaiman & Polon,
Inc., New York City; in Australasia and Southeast
Asia by John Wiley & Sons Australasia Pty. Ltd.,
Sydney; in India by UBS Publishers' Distributors
Pvt., Ltd., Delhi; in Japan by John Weatherhill,
Inc., Tokyo.

Preface to the 1964 Edition

AFTER fifteen years I find myself still in essential agreement with the ideas expressed in this book. I might now try to be more polite—or more charitable —to those who hold other views. It also seems to me that the difficult task to which pages 6-18 are addressed might better have been postponed to a later position in the work. Some readers may wish to skip this passage, at least until they have acquainted themselves with the main message of the book. Perhaps the pages on Bradley (31-36) and the Appendix to Chapter Two (95-115) should be treated in the same way. In spite of the abstractness of some of the reasoning, a good deal of the thought should be intelligible to readers other than technical philosophers.

The question considered in these lectures was not, Does the God of religion exist? but rather, What can most reasonably be meant by the religious term "God"? Since 1947 a host of articles and books have appeared, in this country and in England, dealing with a similar question—often phrased as "the problem of religious language," or "for what job is the word 'God,' and other words closely associated with this one, employed?" It seems to me that these writings are bringing about a somewhat new climate of opinion in which the considerations put forward in this book have a better chance of being understood than they had when I wrote it. For the new demand that more naive forms of religious speech should have precedence over the technicalities of the old religious metaphysics ought to favor recognition of divine relativity (which, as I argue, is not only compatible with, but equivalent to, an aspect of divine absoluteness). True, this too is technical language, but as the reader will find me in effect arguing, it has a far higher

degree of continuity with the naive ways of speaking referred
to than the old identification of the God of worship with "the
absolute" or "the infinite."

Another change since I wrote these lectures is that, whereas
then it seemed that not only the Church of Rome but nearly all
conservative Protestantism was committed to the absolutistic
conception of deity, there are now increasing signs that no
church is irrevocably so committed. I am thinking of some indi-
cations in the writings of numerous theologians, and also of
conversations I have had with a number of Roman Catholic
scholars interested in Whitehead's work, or in that of Peirce,
James, even Dewey—or in mine. Equally important perhaps
is the change in philosophers generally. The violent shocks
administered by Wittgenstein and Heidegger—and violent is
not too strong a word—have had at least this good effect:
that young men are no longer so sure that religion as a live
option is identical with some standard metaphysical position
of the past, so that if this position can be justified so can
religion, and if it can be discredited so can religion as a whole,
or at least, religion as worship of a God existing independ-
ently of man. There is a pervasive sense that the old issues
were more or less ambiguous, not to be taken at face value, and
while I think that our ancestors in some respects made more
sense than most linguistic analysts allow, I also think that at
certain points they failed to do so. I believe they were under
pressures which caused them to employ "systematically misleading expressions"—even though I differ considerably with
the author of this phrase as to the identification of these expressions, and even though I suspect that those who appeal to
this and other similar slogans are themselves not above committing the faults so named, especially when they condescend
to deal with the central religious question. The worst aspect
of the present philosophical scene is the habit of allowing

trivialities to usurp attention while the more substantial issues get only casual notice. But anyone with a bit of courage can still tackle these issues, and with rather less danger than formerly of falling into merely traditional traps. So, on the whole, there may be more, rather than less, speculative freedom now.

In a recent work, *The Logic of Perfection* (Open Court, 1962), I try to show how the relativistic conception of the absoluteness, perfection, or infinity of deity makes it possible to defend the Ontological Argument for God's existence against the standard criticisms. In *Anselm's Discovery*, soon to be published, I complete this line of inquiry, so far as it is in my power to do so. In another largely written book, a systematic metaphysics, further theistic arguments are presented which I believe are significantly different, though distantly related to, the classical proofs commonly said to have been "demolished" by Hume and Kant. I am convinced that "classical theism" (as much Greek as Christian, Jewish, or Islamic) was an incorrect translation of the central religious idea into philosophical categories, and that consequently the failure of the classical proofs which accompanied that mistranslation is like the blowing up of the bridges on a route which at best was a detour and at worst led simply in the wrong direction. The task of evaluating religious belief was not, for today's needs, performed by the men of the Newtonian era. New theological views, radically new views in natural science, new attitudes in philosophy have too greatly transformed the questions. This undertaking cannot be put off upon previous centuries. It will be done anew, or left undone. Neither medieval nor early modern metaphysics (as Kant, for instance, knew the latter in Leibniz and Baumgarten) can any longer serve as the model by which religious metaphysics as such must stand or fall. The past one hundred and fifty years, and especially the past forty years, have seen important developments, which I sometimes refer to under the label "neoclassical metaphysics," or "neo-classical theism." Criticism which ignores such views is unwittingly antiquarian, even though it may employ fashionable devices.

These views are not all exclusively mine, and of course they can be traced back, in vaguer or less complete forms, for centuries. Somewhat similar ideas may be gleaned from Fechner and Lequier—to mention only these two—of the last century, and from Whitehead, Montague, and Berdyaev of ours.

Some of the things said in this book could very likely be said better. But not a great many philosophers are trying to say them at all. That they need saying, I have no doubt.

C. H.

Austin, Texas
July 1963

Preface to the Original Edition

IN THIS book, which is a considerable expansion of the lectures as given, the attempt is made to apply logical analysis to the religious idea of God. One making such an attempt must expect the opposition both of many of the orthodox and of some of their skeptical opponents, holding respectively that the conception of deity is above, or below, the useful application of such analysis. The main thesis, called Surrelativism, also Panentheism, is that the "relative" or changeable, that which depends upon and varies with varying relationships, includes within itself and in value exceeds the nonrelative, immutable, independent, or "absolute," *as the concrete includes and exceeds the abstract.* From this doctrine, the proof for which is chiefly in the second chapter, it follows that God, as supremely excellent and concrete, must be conceived not as wholly absolute or immutable, but rather as supremely-relative, "surrelative," although, or because of this superior relativity, containing an abstract character or essence in respect to which, but only in respect to which, he is indeed strictly absolute and immutable. Thus Surrelativism, although a single logical principle, not an eclectic conjunction of doctrines, synthesizes into a higher unity "relativism"—all [concrete] beings are relative—and "absolutism"—there is a wholly nonrelative [abstract] being. The brackets show the qualifications by which the synthesis is effected. "Divine Relativity," it is maintained, includes all the divine absoluteness (or eternity) that logical analysis shows to be conceivable without sheer contradiction. (Some of the contradictions arising from the traditional doctrine of a wholly absolute deity are exhibited in Chapter I, second and third sections, and in the first section of Chapter II.) In this way the "personal" conception of deity required in religion is reconciled with the requirements of philosophic reason—which indeed, as I argue, is just as much in need of such a conception as is religion. A personal God is one who has social relations, really has them, and thus is constituted by relationships and hence is relative—in a sense not provided for by the traditional doctrine of a divine Substance wholly nonrelative toward the world, though allegedly containing loving relations between the "persons" of the Trinity.

As the long argument between those who said that light was corpuscular and those who said it was a set of waves seems, in our time, to have ended with the admission that it is both, in each case with qualifications; so the longer argument between those who said, There is nothing higher than relative being (and thus either there is no God or he is relative), and those who said, There is a highest being who is absolute, is perhaps to be ended by showing a way in which both statements may consistently be made. As Morris Cohen says, in his *Preface to Logic* [1] (pp. 74–75): "The law of contradiction does not bar the presence of contrary determinations in the same entity, but only requires . . . a distinction of aspects . . . in which the contraries hold." And again, ". . . we must be on our guard against the universal tendency to simplify situations and to analyze them in terms of only one of such contrary tendencies. This principle of polarity is a maxim of research. . . . It may be generalized as the principle . . . of the necessary co-presence and mu-

1. New York, Henry Holt, 1944.

tual dependence of opposite determinations." Surrelativism is the doctrine of absolute and relative that conforms to the polar principle. How "mutual dependence" between absolute and relative is compatible with the independence properly connoted by the former is shown in Chapter II.

The theory is of course not wholly new. From Plato's *Timaeus* through the obscurities of Schelling's *Ages of the World* and the clearer pages of Fechner's *Zend Avesta* (chap. xi) to Whitehead's *Process and Reality* or Montague's *Ways of Things*—or, in more mystical vein, Berdyaev's *Destiny of Man* and Niebuhr's *Human Destiny* (note the second section of chap. iii of that book)—not to mention many other philosophers and theologians of recent times, one can trace its emergence.

In this book I do not conceal my own faith—shared with those just mentioned—that theistic religion, thus reformulated, is true as well as conceivable; but the only bearing of this personal religious belief upon the argument is that it may afford some evidence that theism can avoid logical absurdities and still be a religious doctrine. One may go further, and hold that the severe discipline to which modern logic—stimulated by advances in knowledge, especially mathematics—has been subjecting philosophy can help to free religion from some confusions which are not merely logical but are also emotional and ethical. Had I the training and skill in logic of a Carnap (to whose sharp but impersonal and helpful criticisms I am much indebted) I could demonstrate the soundness of this belief—if it be sound—more convincingly than, as it is, I can expect to do. But there seems to be no one with such equipment who possesses also adequate familiarity with religious thought. It is the usual situation in our age of complex specialization. There are some gratifying signs, however, that to be a technical logician may not much longer, to the same extent as in the recent past, mean to view theology with contempt or despair.

The logical core of surrelativism is mostly in Chapter II, and is a theory of "external" and "internal" relatedness, connected respectively with the absolute and the surrelative aspects of deity. This chapter contains also my criticisms of Absolute Idealism and defends the logical heresy (but medieval commonplace): not every actual relationship has an actual converse, i.e., a relation a R b can be real although the converse relation b R a (for example, "b is known by a," where a does know b) is only nominal, a mere way of speaking. This medieval doctrine I regard as the only valid basis of a realistic theory of knowledge, the true way out of the "ego-centric predicament." Despite the too polemical tone of my references to classical theology, especially Thomism, I am obviously indebted to this tradition—perhaps almost as much as to Whitehead, whose views are so much closer to those affirmed in this book. To have stated with precision and completeness what nearly everyone else had long been holding more vaguely and confusedly, is a high merit in philosophy, no matter how incorrect may be what is stated—and who has possessed this merit in greater degree than Thomas of Aquin? Our gratitude may not be measured by our agreement. For if, as I believe, his doctrine was shipwrecked on certain rocks of contradiction, has he not left us an admirable chart showing the location of the rocks!

Surrelativism, as remarked above, is a single tenet (regarding the relations of absolute and relative) not an eclectic assemblage of tenets. Nevertheless, it can appeal to the following authorities for support of its various corollaries: to modern pluralists, such as G. E. Moore, R. B. Perry, and William James, and contemporary logicians generally, in behalf of external relations (better, external relatedness, for the same relation may be external to one term and internal to another); to Thomas Aquinas in behalf of the identification of absolute (or independent and immutable) with externally related; to both modern and medieval realists—save as the latter were guilty of abandoning their principle when treating of deity—in behalf of the view that a particular or actual knowing, even in the divine instance, must depend upon and internally have relation to the thing known, while the latter does not, in general, depend upon being object of any particular knowing. Further, the conception of a relative nature in God can be associated to some extent with two influential trends of today, Existentialism and Crisis Theology. In concrete or surrelative aspect, God, like all existents, has qualities that are accidental, that do not follow from any necessity of his essence. This is, of course, in so far an existentialist tenet, though applied, as Existentialists refuse to apply it, to deity. Further, that man is, in some degree, self-created (Sartre) is a corollary of surrelativist or panentheist theism (cf. Whitehead's "self-created creature"). With Crisis Theology, which in a fashion is existential, our theory can agree that God is personal and self-related to the creatures, and that his acts of self-relationship are not rationally deducible, but require to be "encountered." However, as Barth and Brunner seem not to see, this is compatible with there being an essence of God which is philosophically explicable and knowable. The concrete volitions of God may be contingent or "arbitrary" (not that they do not express goodness, but that goodness has more than one possible expression in a given case) ; nevertheless, contingency or arbitrariness, as such, is not itself arbitrary but a necessary, or a priori, and intelligible category. For each man, indeed, religion is a matter of the actions of God as self-related to him, that is, to a wholly contingent being, or to humanity, likewise contingent. Relations whose terms are contingent can only be contingent. Philosophy seeks that general principle or essence of the divine being of which such concrete actions of God are mere contingent illustrations. But from a religious point of view, it is the illustrations that count. Thus the religious and the philosophical attitudes are complementary, not conflicting. Our doctrine appears, then, to effect a peculiarly comprehensive synthesis of past and present thought concerning theism.

The crucial question is whether or not the synthesis is consistent. It certainly avoids some of the inconsistencies classically charged against theism, but are there perhaps new ones, peculiar to surrelativism? Consistency is here hard to prove, since the proof by exhibition of an actual instance (the only conclusive method known to logic) would in this case mean exhibiting God himself. However, in a sense perhaps this can be done. I intend to devote a book—dealing with the arguments for the divine existence—to the attempt. Meanwhile, I content myself with asking, where is there contradiction in the doctrine as defined, taken in its own terms?

Since this is an essay in metaphysics, some remarks should be made concerning the now fashionable dictum, all knowledge is to be gained by the "empirical method" of science. The first remark is that many able philosophers and logicians do not accept the dictum, in any sense which would clearly exclude metaphysics as distinctive in method (e.g., C. I. Lewis—chap. i of *Mind and the World Order*—E. J. Nelson, and others). The second remark is that mathematics has a partially different method from that of the concrete or special sciences, and that the justification for this difference is parallel to one which can be given for a distinctive procedure in metaphysics. Mathematics has a distinctive method because it deals with entities, for example, numbers, which are of different "logical type" from concrete things or events. The principle here is: A logical difference justifies a methodological difference. Now metaphysical doctrines seem to be of different logical type from all others, unless indeed mathematics and logic are compelled, as some authorities hold, to accept a metaphysical principle, such as "It is a necessary or a priori truth that there are real individuals." Apart from such a view, which would apparently make mathematics and logic a part of metaphysics, we may divide knowledge as follows: mathematics, dealing with various "*possible* worlds," or better, various *possible* logical structures; natural and social science, dealing with the one *actual* world; metaphysics, dealing with what is common and *necessary* to all possible states of affairs and all possible truth, including adjudication of the question whether "there is no world at all" represents a conceivable truth or is mere nonsense or contradiction. Now God is conceived as the actual creator of the actual world and the potential creator of possible worlds (according to theism, they could only exist if he created them), or as, through his omniscience, the measure of all actual and possible truth; hence divinity is not a mere fact or fiction of the actual world, but is either nonsense, in relation to all possible states of affairs, or a necessary reality, in the same relation, that is, the idea is metaphysical.

The question of theism thus logically calls for a distinctive method, as compared to that of what is ordinarily called science. Merely to assert that no such method can be valid is to beg the question of theism, not to argue it.

Whether and how we can distinguish between metaphysics and logic is more difficult to say. I am not sure that they do differ. It seems easy to show that logicians today disagree on what are plainly metaphysical questions (referring to what is common to all possibility) : such as, Is all truth eternal? Is there an a priori principle of causal connectedness? Is "some world exists" true not merely in fact, but necessarily, or in any possible case? In this book I am trying to set forth the logic of basic theological concepts ; but perhaps these are the same as the theistic implications of basic logical concepts. If only a few logicians could be induced to look into the matter! On one point, at least, I believe metaphysics can agree with contemporary logic : metaphysical truths, if valid, must since they are to be necessary be "analytic," if that means, "certified by meaning alone." I am confident that the theistic question will be rationally settled when, if ever, it becomes really clear to educated persons what are the possible consistent meanings, if any, of "supreme being," "absolute," "perfect," "necessary being," and the like. To hasten that time is the main object of this study.

Concerning the present political plight of the world, which often makes one wonder with what right one can yield to the fascination of metaphysical problems, something is said toward the end of the book. Here I wish to express gratitude toward those, including multitudes of Russians (who may not have intended just this effect, to be sure) whose recent sacrifices make it still possible to discuss philosophical problems with intellectual honesty, without interference from persons who would like to silence or suborn those with whom they are not competent to argue. The doctrine of divine relativity is not entirely unconnected with the great drive toward a synthesis of freedom and order which, as Heimann reminds us, is our political goal. God orders the universe, according to panentheism, by taking into his own life all the currents of feeling in existence. He is the most irresistible of influences precisely because he is himself the most open to influence. In the depths of their hearts all creatures (even those able to "rebel" against him) defer to God because they sense him as the one who alone is adequately moved by what moves them. He alone not only knows but feels (the only adequate knowledge, where feeling is concerned) how they feel, and he finds his own joy in sharing their lives, lived according to their own free decisions, not fully anticipated by any detailed plan of his own. Yet the extent to which they can be permitted to work out their own plan depends on the extent to which they can echo or imitate on their own level the divine sensitiveness to the needs and precious freedom of all. In this vision of a deity who is not a supreme autocrat, but a universal agent of "persuasion," whose "power is the worship he inspires" (Whitehead), that is, flows from the intrinsic appeal of his infinitely sensitive and tolerant relativity, by which all things are kept moving in orderly togetherness, we may find help in facing our task of today, the task of contributing to the democratic self-ordering of a world whose members not even the supreme orderer reduces to mere subjects with the sole function of obedience. If even God thinks enough of the least and worst of us to permit us to form, with all that we are, integral self-determined members of his present reality, rivulets poured into his "ocean of feeeling," it ought not to be beneath our human condescension toward each other to accord that "respect for the human individual" (or still better, that Reverence for Life—Schweitzer) which contemporary thought acclaims as the universal ethical standard.

I am grateful (and the reader may be grateful) to Dorothy C. Hartshorne for editing manuscript and proofs. I also feel indebted to Paul Weiss for generous encouragement; to Yale University for furnishing the occasion of this writing; and to members of the seminar of faculty and graduate students—which my colleague, then chairman, Charner Perry, so wisely instituted, several years ago, in our department of philosophy—for criticisms upon portions of the manuscript read or summarized before them.

CONTENTS

THE DIVINE RELATIVITY

CHAPTER I

God as Supreme, Yet Indebted to All

CAN the idea of deity be so formulated as to preserve, perhaps even increase, its religious value, while yet avoiding the contradictions which seem inseparable from the idea as customarily defined? To show that this can be done is the aim of the present work. By religious value I mean the power to express and enhance reverence or worship on a high ethical and cultural level. The question is whether and how God (or, if you prefer, the Supreme Being) can be conceived without logical absurdity, and as having such a character that an enlightened person may worship and serve him with whole heart and mind.

The problem of the existence of a supreme being I shall not discuss on this occasion. It deserves a study to itself. But unless "supreme" or "divine" or "perfect" can in some sense be conceived, it is useless to speak of proofs for such a being. How could we logically establish an intrinsically illogical conclusion! Yet theologians have rather generally admitted that the idea of God, as formulated by them, involves insuperable paradoxes. We are even told that a God conceivable without paradox would not be God. Admittedly a being conceivable through and through without mystery, in the sense of aspects inaccessible to our knowledge, would not be God. But what, in this connection, is meant by paradox? A theological paradox, it appears, is what a contradiction becomes when it is about God rather than something else, or indulged in by a theologian or a church rather than an unbeliever or a heretic. That many of the traditional paradoxes are downright contradictions we shall show later. Even those philosophers who have rejected every idea of God have generally done so on the assumption that any such idea must be construed in the customary contradictory manner. If we are to discuss the religious question rationally, we must be willing to explore impartially the alternative ways of relating the object of worship to philosophical concepts, such as "absolute," "immutable," "uncaused," "aseity," and the like—if and where necessary, redefining or qualifying these conceptions to remove any contradictions they would otherwise involve. Unfortunately, even when thinkers do free themselves from the assumption that religion must stand or fall, intellectually, with the customary paradoxical definitions, they often fall into the opposite extreme of denying any connection of the religious idea with the philosophical technicalities mentioned, thus yielding the notion of a God wholly relative, mutable, and emergent. But that there is *some* connection of the religious idea with the terms previously listed is too evident for their abandonment to be justified, unless after the possible ways of construing them have been fairly exhausted. And there is *one* such way that was almost never definitely thought of prior to Schelling, and is usually not clearly envisaged even yet, either by believers or by unbelievers. To explain this neglected possibility is the chief end of the present undertaking.

If we can free the idea of the supreme being from absurdity, we shall have at least a partial answer to those positivists who declare that metaphysical ideas are without intellectual import. For surely one chief reason for their thinking so is the admitted tendency of these ideas to generate antinomies; and the idea of deity is the chief, if not (as I believe) the sum, of the metaphysical ideas.

Also, if the ontological argument is valid in some form, an affirmative answer to the question Is there a God? follows logically from an affirmative answer to the question Is a God conceivable? The issue here is whether or not the existence of deity is, at least in one aspect, of a logically different type from that of other entities; an issue which is begged if the "empirical criterion of meaning" is applied without proper qualifications.

Logical and Metaphysical Paradoxes

We live in an age in which logicians and mathematicians have been struggling, with at least partial success, to remove paradoxes associated with the foundations of mathematics, itself the foundation of all science. In view of this, we might well hesitate before accepting the assumption that the metaphysico-theological paradoxes are incurable. Perhaps they are merely unavoidable with customary logical techniques, but avoidable with more refined techniques. In logic the difficulties have, in certain ways, been overcome, but not without an upheaval in thought-habits, an upheaval which to some may perhaps seem as objectionable as any paradox. And it is obvious that the resistance to a similar upheaval in metaphysics is bound to be greater. Even the opponents, perhaps especially the opponents, of traditional metaphysics would be embarrassed if it turned out that metaphysicians really could talk sense if they tried hard enough and changed their ways enough.

The analogy between the metaphysical and the logical paradoxes is perhaps fairly close; for in both cases, as I shall try to show, what is required is that we take account of differences in "logical type" or level, or at any rate in degree of abstraction, and not pass, for instance, from concrete particulars to universals, or from thoughts of first intention to those of second intention, as in going from classes of individuals to classes of classes of individuals, without due precautions. If this is so, the famous paradoxes, or contradictions—to avoid the customary euphemism—of metaphysics and theology are not, as is claimed, the inevitable result of human limitations, of the finite or relative or conditioned trying to understand the infinite or absolute or unconditioned, nor of the meaninglessness of the latter, but the natural yet avoidable result of haste and inattention to exact shades of meaning. These errors have unfortunately become habitual, partly through inertia, pride of opinion, or undue deference to tradition, partly through ecclesiastical tyranny—to avoid another euphemism—and partly through a false humility which fears to offend or do injustice to deity by exerting our human powers of analysis to the utmost in regard to sacred matters. The humility is false, since to analyze, argue, infer—as theologians certainly did—and yet perform these operations carelessly or incorrectly can hardly be an appropriate way of honoring the creator of human reason. And if paradoxes are not accepted as signs that we are thinking badly, what sign would we recognize? The very people who choose the soft words, paradox and mystery, for what, so far as they have shown, are simply contradictions in their own thinking, resort to the harsher terms, absurdity or contradiction, do they not, when they meet with difficulties not essentially different in systems which they oppose? Furthermore, Feuerbach brilliantly showed that to the orthodox explanation of theological paradox in terms of the incomprehensible greatness of God there is a promising atheistic alternative, according to which the paradox results from the erroneous attribution to the nonhuman, the cosmos, of what are really human traits, such as thought or will, taken purely generally or in abstraction from the particular limitations of concrete human beings. I do not say that Feuerbach's procedure is wholly legitimate; but I do suggest that an illogical position is hardly strengthened by the apparent logic with which it furnishes reasons for its own illogicality. If the truth of the position implies that it must be illogical, it would seem the untruth (absurdity) of the position is likely to imply it even more clearly.

To prevent misconception, I should add the following. There is much, in a sense infinitely much, that we cannot know about the universe and God; but, as I shall try to show, it does not lie in any insolubility in principle of the conceptual problem of infinite and finite, or of absolute and relative. Either "absolute" is our own human concept, or we have no right to use the word; if it is our concept, it is our responsibility to fix its meaning. Knowing the meaning of absolute, and of relative, we cannot fail to know the relations of these conceptual meanings to each other; for nothing determines these relations but just the meanings themselves. It is in another direction that we must look for impenetrable theological mystery. And there is no lack of it.

It really does not help to say that absolute is a merely negative term, meaning nonrelative, and is thus a denial of human meaning, not itself such a meaning. "Not" is also a human meaning; the sense in which relativity can consistently be negated must be inherent in the concept of relativity. We have only to discover this sense and adhere to it and the paradoxes become merely, like those in the logic of classes, difficulties which require great pains to overcome, and which perhaps can be overcome only by sacrificing certain methods of thinking, or of speaking, which for some purposes are very convenient.

External Relations and Knowledge

Let us see what the paradoxes in question are. They appear in many forms, of which I mention a few. To think is to relate. For thought, then, reality is something "relative" or relational. Yet if we try to think of *everything* as relative there seem to be difficulties. For instance, if all things are relative, if they depend upon and vary with varying relationships, then at least relativity itself, and as such (and perhaps other abstractions) must be something invariant, nonrelative, or "absolute." Or again, if—as in physics—simultaneity is relative to a frame of reference, still, given the frame of reference, or viewing the simultaneity as including the required relativity, we seem, taking the theory at face value, to have something not relative to anything further, and in so far absolute. There are, of course, other ways, less simple, but perhaps more cogent, of arguing for the conclusion that not literally "everything" can be relative, but that something must be absolute. On the other hand, if—as most philosophers and nearly all theologians have maintained—something is absolute, how can this something be object of our thought? To be something referred to, even as "unknown" or mysterious, is not that to be in relation? And is not all thought comparison, and is not comparison a positing of relations? Or, has not the absolute always been thought of as the cause or ground of all things, and is not the cause in relation to its effects? Unless, then, it is possible to be "in relation" without in any way becoming "relative," without the relations qualifying the things said to be terms of these relations, there can, it seems, be no intelligible treatment of either relativity or absoluteness. But can a thing be in relation and yet exactly as it would be were it not in relation? In other language, can there be relations "external" to their terms, or at least to one of these, so that the term in no way "depends" for its being or nature upon the relations?

Such nonintrinsic, nonconstitutive, external relations were standard doctrine in the Middle Ages. A curious example is that if an animal stands to the left of a pillar, the animal is really related to the pillar, but not the pillar to the animal. There is some point to the example, in that the animal may actually adjust to the pillar, perceive the latter's position and choose the relation in which it will stand to it, so that its quality of experience is definitely qualified by relation to the pillar, whereas nothing similar is obvious concerning the pillar's relation to the animal. I wish to signalize the fact that it is the animal's superiority that renders it more relative, or at least more conspicuously relative, than the inanimate pillar. I believe the same could be shown with respect to other scholastic illustrations, even that of a man and his shadow. It is *qua* unconscious of his shadow that a man is unmodified by relation to it. An automobile is even more nonrelative to its shadow than a waking man. And the reason our awareness of the shadow only slightly relativizes us to it is that we are cognitively relative to a vastly larger world. It was indeed the Thomistic doctrine that in knowledge, apart from God, it is the knower who is really related to the known, not the known to the knower. This constitutes a point of agreement between medieval and current realism. In knowing, we enjoy relation to things that are what they are without regard to the fact that we know them. Thus the cognitive relation is external to the known, internal to the knower. Moreover, in so far as relations are known, they cannot be external to the mind that knows them. For, in having knowledge, mind has the cognitive relation, and in knowing some *other* relation, it has this other relation as term of its cognitive relation. Thus mind has all relations, at least so far as they are known. Finally, in cases (if there are such) where a relation is external to *all* its terms, the only "place" where the relation can have its being is "in the mind." So the usual description of relations that are regarded as not really in things has been that they are "relations of reason," relations that are there only for the beholding and comparing mind. Thus all roads seem to lead to the conclusion that mind or awareness is the most relational or relative of all things. If, then, anything is absolute, it seems that it cannot be mind. Nothing is so variously relative, dependent, as the knower.

In the foregoing theory of knowledge, medieval doctrine and twentieth-century realism seem to agree—with the sole and startling exception that medieval theory reverses the principle when the discussion turns to God. God knows all things, but in such fashion (it was held) that there is zero relativity or dependence in God as knower, and maximal dependence in the creatures as known. Divine thought is the sheer opposite of thought in general, in that it endows its terms with all their being and nature. The divine knowledge creates all things, but itself derives nothing from them as created. It is this alleged *reversal* of cognitive relativity in God that I wish to challenge.

But surely, it will be said, human knowledge is not the model for divine knowledge. Human knowledge may be relative; but divine knowledge is divine exactly because it is absolute, not relative. My reply is: (1) divine knowledge is indeed divine because it is absolute, but I shall demonstrate that not only does this not mean that it is in every respect absolute, but it even implies that the divine is relative in all but one aspect; (2) the notion that our knowledge is relative solely *because of its inferiority* is largely wrong. On the contrary, the fallibility and incompleteness of our knowledge consists in the drastically restricted scope of cer-

tain aspects of its relativity; (3) it is precisely the ideal
case of knowledge, knowledge absolute in certainty and
complete adequacy to the known, that must in some other
aspects be literally and unrestrictedly relative. Let us be-
gin with the last point. Infallible, certain, distinct, and
complete knowledge of reality is knowledge in which something corresponds to and implies each and every item of
reality. If any item, in fact certainly known to exist, had
not existed, the knowledge that it exists would have been
absent from the infallible knowledge, and the knowledge of
the alternative state of reality, in fact absent from the
knowledge, would have been present. Infallible knowledge
is something which, being itself known, all other things are
known. Thus whoever knows (as God himself, at least,
might know) the truth of "God knows infallibly that
there are men" will certainly know as true "there are
men." The first proposition strictly implies or entails the
second. Now we may define relativity or dependence as "the
ontological correlate of the logical relation of entailment."
This definition is rendered more precise in Chapter II. A
term to which a relation is external or nonrelativizing is a
term whose being can be fully asserted in propositions none
of which entails the assertion of the relatum. Since "God
knows there are men" entails "there are men," that in God
to which the first proposition refers is relative, not nonrelative or absolute, with respect to that to which the second
proposition refers. If these definitions be objected to, my
opponent may be challenged to produce any definite unambiguous, alternative definition which will be compatible
with the conception of a wholly nonrelative and yet infallible knowledge.

Now for point (2). Not every alternative in the world
implies an alternative state in human knowledge, or in other
words, the state of our knowledge does not entail the exact

state of the world. My feelings and beliefs give no unambiguous information about the rest of the world. He who knows that I believe (and think I know) that there are electrons does not, merely from that, have knowledge that in fact there are electrons. Perhaps some slight probability would be established, but that is apparently all. Or suppose I believe that I know that an acquaintance is honest in a business proposal. For all that he may be dishonest. People thus have a good deal of independence or nonrelativity with respect to the things existing for them to know. They can believe in what is not there to believe in; they can fail to believe in what is there to believe in. And if you say this is belief, not knowledge, the point is that internally it is much the same, and you would have to inspect more than the state of mind to know for certain how far the belief is true. Unrestricted or literal relativity, so far from being the mere *de facto* character of our inferior human knowledge, is rather the precise ideal of knowledge in its most absolute meaning. It is divine knowledge that cannot believe in the existence of what is not existent, or fail to believe—that is, be aware of as existing—in what does exist. That human knowledge is approximate and probable seems to mean that it is neither exactly relative to the world to be known, nor wholly independent of this world, but something in between. In this middling or unstrict character of our cognitive relativity, not in the fact that it is relative, lies our deficiency. And the less we are in a position to have knowledge of something, the looser seem to be our ties of dependence upon it. We approach strict dependence in proportion as our knowledge is distinct and immediate. Thus we cannot directly intuit a pattern of color qualities without this pattern's constituting also a part of the pattern of our immediate experience in its unity as an experience. As the intuited pattern changes, so the character of that unitary experience changes. Ducasse, Parker, and others have—I dare to think—demonstrated this. Since everyone holds that God's knowledge is intuitive not inferential, certain not probable, with respect to the entire universe, it is, once more, precisely the divine knowledge whose pattern or character must "depend" (in the sense of our definition) the most extensively upon the universe.

It is entirely neutral to this argument whether, or in what sense, divine knowledge creates its objects. The point is, what knowledge the divine has must be one thing if it creates (or if there exists) *this* world, and another thing if it creates *that* world. For the one knowledge will be such that its description entails "there is such and such a world"; the other that its description entails, "there is not a world of the previously specified character, but only one of another character." Entities whose descriptions imply contradictory consequences cannot be one and the same entity. Therefore God's knowledge differentially implies, and thus in our defined sense is relative to, the actual state of *all* existence, i.e., its relativity is unrestricted in scope.

As to point (1), since it is the main thesis of this book, it cannot be elucidated here. But I may remark that "God is infallible" does not entail "there are men." Accordingly, God's possession of infallibility, as such, is wholly independent of, nonrelative to, contingent existents. All that is relative in God is whether he shall have infallible knowledge that there is such and such a world, or infallible knowledge that there is some other sort of world instead. The concrete knowledge is relative, the generic abstract property of being-all-knowing is strictly absolute. There will be more of this in the following chapters, in which points (2) and (3) will also be further developed. We shall see, too, that the divine relativity not only does not contradict the creative power of the divine knowing, but alone renders it intelligible (see Chapter III).

An historic argument for reversed cognitive relativity in the case of deity is that, whereas our knowledge is "measured"—as to truth—by its objects, God is his own and the ultimate measure of truth. The answer is: God is the measure of truth, as we are not, because he and only he is able to establish a perfect correspondence between his knowing and what he knows, or between what he knows it to be and what it is. Now this correspondence implies relativity and contingency on the divine side regardless of whether it is exclusively God who causes things to conform to his knowledge, or in part also things which influence the knowing to conform to them. For the point is that another universe was possible (if anything at all is contingent), and that the identical knowledge cannot, on pain of contradiction, agree with alternative universes. Infallible knowledge that world W is actual, world W^1 only possible, is logically incompatible with the inactuality of W and with the actuality of W^1. Hence if this knowledge be necessary, then that with which it is incompatible, the inactuality of W or the actuality of W^1, are impossible absolutely, and the real world is as necessary as God, and there are no "possible worlds" in any sense. Supposing the knowing to determine the objects rather than vice versa has no effect on the logic of the case. Consider the following:

1. If and only if W is actual, God knows it is actual.
2. If and only if God knows W is actual, it is actual.

Those who deny that the known determines or conditions the knowing in the divine instance may reject (1), as implying such conditioning. But any logician can see that there is no difference between (1) and (2), and in any event (2) makes the divine cognition subject to contingency, to an "if," even more plainly, if possible, than (1). And should it be denied that the "if" really means the possibility of the contradictory, then the divine knowing that W is actual must be taken as necessary, and therefore that which is logically inseparable from or entailed by it, that W is actual, must be held exactly as necessary, and nothing is left to constitute the referent of contingent or possible, and therewith "necessary" as applied to deity loses all distinctive meaning.

Another formulation is the following:

Let W be a certain kind of world

Let P be the proposition: "God knows W exists"

Let Q be the proposition: "W exists"

Axiom: P -Q impossible. (The conjunction of P and the negation of Q involves contradiction, since what is divinely, i.e., infallibly, known to be true cannot be false.)

Thesis to be refuted (by *reductio ad absurdum*) : "P is necessarily true," or "-P impossible."

Proof: Since P -Q is impossible (axiom), and since (thesis) -P is also impossible, the only permissible joint truth values are P Q. Hence P and Q are both necessary in the same sense, there being no alternative to either. In every way, the logical status of Q becomes indistinguishable from that attributed to P. If P -Q is impossible, no less so is Q -P. For assuming, as the thesis implies, that an omniscient being exists, a proposition cannot be true without God's knowing that it is true; and besides, Q -P must be impossible if -P itself is impossible. But again, if -P is impossible, it follows that -Q is equally so. For -Q entails the disjunction: -Q P v -Q -P; but the first is impossible (axiom), and if -P is impossible, -Q -P is equally so. Altogether, P and Q function alike logically, and on the assumption that P is necessary, Q must be construed as necessary in the same sense.

What is proved above is not simply that, assuming P to be true, the truth of Q follows; but rather, assuming P to be necessarily true, it follows that Q is also and in the same sense a necessarily true proposition. To say, then, as the view I combat does, that God is a "necessary being," in a sense in which the world is not (otherwise, nothing distinctive is conveyed by "necessary"), and that *qua* necessary he knows the world to exist as not necessary, is to utter purely emotional or simply nonsensical language, void of logical significance, hence of intellectual import. It simply cannot be that everything in God is necessary, including his knowledge that this world exists, unless the world is in the same sense necessary and there is no contingency whatever. In that case, necessity contrasts with nothing and says nothing. Therewith the thesis to be refuted is shown empty of consistent meaning.

What does have such meaning is the contradictory proposition, "-P is possible," or in other terms, "God's knowing that such and such a world exists is a contingent knowing," i.e., the proposition denying such knowledge could be true. The possible truth values are still such as not to distinguish P and Q as to logical status; but now the values are P Q and also -P -Q, and thus the contingency of the world becomes assertible, -Q being recognized as possible. Moreover, as we shall see more clearly later, it becomes legitimate to affirm that deity exists necessarily, in a sense in which men, for example, do not, even though not all the factors in God—for example, his actual cognitions—can be necessary. P and Q indeed function alike; but certain propositions other than P, yet descriptive of God, function otherwise. For example, "God knows as actual whatever is

actual." This proposition (let us call it P′) is not only
different from P, it is compatible with -P, as well as with
-Q. To deduce P from P′ we must have the further and contingent premise, "W exists or is actual." From this we see
—and it is a bit hard to understand how it could ever have
been overlooked or denied—that God as designated by the
two propositions P and P′ cannot be in all respects identical.
Here are two modally diverse, not logically equivalent,
propositions about God, which cannot both be necessary.
It follows—I think follows rigorously—that there must be
two really distinct aspects of the divine being, supposing
God to exist, both of which cannot be necessary, although
one of them may be so. It is this two-aspect doctrine which,
as I hope to show, solves the traditional theistic paradoxes.

Let us consider more closely the manner in which the
great theologians of the past dealt with the absolute-
relative problem. God, they said (not without misgivings,
to be sure), is absolute and totally exempt from relations to
the creatures. One might quote Philo, Aquinas,[1] and many
others. On the other hand, it was admitted that the absolute
being or essence of God, what he is in himself, is unknown
to us, apart from revelation. What we know rationally is
only God as cause of the world. But how can we know God
as causally related to the world, if he is not related at all, if
he has no relative being? If God is purely absolute, then the
being which he enjoys simply in himself is his *only* being,
and if this cannot be known, then it seems we can know or
think *nothing* of God, either as he is in himself or not as he
is in himself.

Of course, one might say that although we cannot know
God-related-to-the-world we can perhaps know the-world-

1. See *Sum. Theol.*, I.a.q.13: a.7.c; cf. 1 *Dist.*, 30 q.1: a.3. sol; *Con. Gen.*,
lib. II, cap. 12.

related-to-God. Or, God is a term, but not a subject, of relationships. It is the world, but not God, which is qualified by the relation of "creation." Now the distinction between term and subject of relations I shall try to show is indeed valid. But unfortunately for traditional theologies the distinction is inapplicable to most of the relations which theology is accustomed to posit between God and the world. Consider the following analogy.

By writing certain books, Plato may be said to have "produced" various effects upon subsequent philosophers. But these relations of causation to the later philosophers are not to be imagined as elements in the being of Plato as he was during his earthly life. Plato was of course conscious that later thinkers would be different because he had written, but he was not conscious that among these thinkers would be Leibnitz and Kant, nor that their reactions to his writings would be just such and such. These relations were not in his experience. Please observe, however, that if Plato could have been aware of his successors, in all their individuality, then their relations to the Platonic writings *would* have qualified Plato's experience. It was just Plato's ignorance of Leibnitz and Kant which made him independent of relationship to them. And it was the knowledge, direct or indirect, which Leibnitz and Kant had of Plato's writings which related them to these writings. Theologians are not content to say that the world is produced or caused by God; they wish also to assert that it is willed, known, and even loved by him. If, then, God is wholly absolute, a term but never a subject of relations, it follows that God does not know or love or will us, his creatures. At most, we can say only that we are known, loved, and willed by him. Here all analogy fails us. "I am loved by you, but it is untrue that you love me"—does this strange combination of words mean anything, even if we suppose them addressed to deity?

All our experience supports the view that the cognitive relation, still more obviously, if possible, a relation such as love, is genuinely constitutive of the knower or the lover, rather than of the known or loved. True, we all like to be loved, but that is because we can be aware of being loved. Is it anything to a picture that someone admires it? Or to the Pythagorean theorem that a certain child enjoys studying it, or dislikes studying it? It is awareness that enables relations to make a difference to a thing. Merely being-known or being-loved is nothing to a thing; but knowing that one is known or loved—that may be a great deal. The conclusion is very simple. The purely absolute God was, by logical implication, conceived as a thing, not a subject or a person; as ignorant, not conscious and knowing; as indifferent, not interested in things and their relations.

Please note that in knowing Plato, what Leibnitz knows is precisely the Plato that is *not* relative to Leibnitz, but absolute with reference to him. True he knows this Plato imperfectly, but to deny he knows Plato leads to a self-contradictory notion that our ideas of our predecessors are ideas of our ideas, etc. "Plato so far as known to us" is meaningless unless it means that much of what Plato was (and would have been had we never known him) which we happen to know. If Plato *has* no relativity to us, then we cannot know any such relativity. Our knowledge can be as relative to ourselves as you please, but what we know, so far as we know Plato at all, is just Plato. Similarly with God. Either he has relative being, and then we might know it, or if he has only absolute being, then the only God we can know in the least is the absolute God in his absoluteness.

To say, we know, not God, but something to which we know that God is analogous, does not meet my argument. Analogy involves relation, thus:—"We know there is Something to which the world is related as effect to cause."

If the relation is in God, then he is relative. If it is in the world, then the world has relation-to-God, and since this is a complex which includes God, and since God has, by hypothesis, only absolute being, the world must include this absolute being. Otherwise, what the world has is not relation-to-God, but relation-to, and nowhere, in the world or in God, is there any such relation as the analogy involves. So "the analogy of being" fails to provide an answer to the question, what do we know when we know God?

Even if the reasoning in the two previous paragraphs be rejected, the more important point stands that it is *as* ignorant that Plato is absolute in relation to Leibnitz and *as* knowing and so far as knowing that Leibnitz is relative to Plato. Therefore, if knowledge is a merit, especially knowledge in its ideal case of infallible certainty, then to be absolute and only absolute is to lack this merit.

Nonidentity of Supreme and Absolute

Of course one is free to mean by "absolute" whatever is supreme or most excellent. But then one is not free to use the same word, without warning, for the nonrelative, for what is independent, immutable, impassive, and the like. It is not self-evident that independence (or immutability) as such *is* excellence, and that excellence as such *is* independence. On the contrary, as I hope in this first chapter to show, excellence or value has a dimension of dependence as well as of independence, and there is no basis for the venerable doctrine that supreme independence will constitute supreme excellence of every kind. To resolve the paradoxes connected with the contrast between relative and absolute we must, I shall argue, admit that "the absolute" is not identical with the supreme being or God, but in a strict sense is infinitely less than the supreme, and in fact is a certain kind of constituent within it. If this admission seems as much a paradox as any which it is designed to remove, the reason is that sufficient attention has not been paid to the definition of "absolute" as simply "what is nonrelative." Why must the nonrelative be more than, or even as much as, the relative? Why must a mere term be more than or equal to a term which involves relations, and hence other terms as relata?

But, it will be said, by God we mean, or for religion we require, not simply a supreme or most excellent but a perfect being. And how can a perfect being change (as it must if relations to the changing world are internal to it)? This argument I counter with a dilemma.

The perfect being either does, or does not, include the totality of imperfect things. If it does, then it is inferior to a conceivable perfection whose constituents would be more perfect. (There is no meaning to the idea of a greatest possible totality of imperfect things.) If the perfect does *not* include the totality of imperfect things, then the total reality which is "the perfect *and* all existing imperfect things" is a greater reality than the perfect alone. If it be said that the perfect, though it does not include the imperfect things, does include their values, whatever is good in them, the reply is that the existence of the imperfect must then be strictly valueless, adding nothing to the sum of values, and might exactly as well not be as be. He who says this implies that God did no good thing when he created the world, and that our human existence is metaphysically useless and meaningless. The only way to escape this is to admit that the perfect-*and*-the-imperfect is something superior to the perfect "alone"—or as independent of the imperfect.

Definition of Perfection

Which horn of this dilemma shall we grasp? If perfection is defined as that which in no respect could conceivably be greater, and hence is incapable of increase, then we face paradox on either hand. But suppose we define the perfect, or supremely excellent or good, as that individual being (in what sense "individual" will appear later) than which no *other individual* being could *conceivably* be greater, but which *itself*, in another "state," could become greater (perhaps by the creation within itself of new constituents). Otherwise expressed, let us define perfection as an excellence such that rivalry or superiority on the part of other individuals is impossible, but self-superiority is not impossible. Or again, let us say that the perfect is the "self-surpassing surpasser of all." This formula resolves the dilemma. For suppose the self-surpassing surpasser of all has the power of unfailingly enjoying as its own constituents whatever imperfect things come to exist. Then it will be bound to possess in its own unity all the values which the imperfect things severally and separately achieve, and therefore it is bound to surpass each and every one of them. Thus it is certain of superiority to any "other individual." It must, in any conceivable state of existence, be the "most excellent being."

By speaking of the perfect as "enjoying" the values of things, I mean to exclude the idea of a mere collection of all things. The surpasser of all others must be a single individual enjoying as his own all the values of all other individuals, and incapable of failing to do so. For this, it is enough to suppose that the being is bound to have adequate knowledge of events when and as they occur, and thereafter. For adequately to know values is to possess them; and to surpass the values of other beings it is enough to possess the values of every one of them from the time these values exist. There is no need to possess them in advance of the others; or to possess them eternally, unless a being which surveys all time eternally is itself a conceivable being—which this essay

seeks to disprove. To surpass other conceivable beings, there
is no need to surpass inconceivable beings, as they would be
if they were, which they are not, conceivable. Even the least
of beings surpasses mere nonsense.

I shall hope to show in this chapter that religion does not
need perfection in any other sense than that called for by
our formula. (If my use of the term "perfection" be objected to, I ask that the phrase "transcendent excellence"
be mentally substituted. I would have used "transcendence"
were it not usually contrasted to immanence, a contrast
here not directly relevant. And I know of no term except
"perfect" which connotes superiority to all possible others.)
Meanwhile, I wish to point out that, although the self-
surpassing surpasser of all must obviously be in some aspect
relative, it does not follow that it is in *no* aspect absolute.
For to be capable of self-increase in *some* respect does not
imply capacity to increase in every respect. Indeed, it is
logically self-evident that in two respects such increase is
excluded by our definition. To be absolutely guaranteed
superiority to absolutely every other individual that comes
to exist is an absolute maximum in certainty and universality of superiority. Moreover, this certainty and universality are intelligible only in terms of such attributes as
omniscience (ideal knowledge), and we shall see that as
"relational types" these are absolute in the strictest sense.

The absolute aspect of perfection, as above defined, may
be symbolized as A-perfection. The relative aspect corre-
spondingly becomes R-perfection. The common element of
"perfection," neutral as between A and R, is "surpasses all
others in all conceivable states of existence."

Since the relativity of the all-surpassing is a unique and
supreme case, it needs a special title. I propose the terms,
Surrelative and Surrelativism, for this kind of relativity
and the doctrine asserting it. The letter R has the con-

venience of being able to suggest another feature of the theory, which is that the relativity of the surrelative is also the reflexivity of its all-surpassingness. It surpasses itself, as well as everything else; with the difference that it surpasses others simultaneously, but itself only in a subsequent state.

Is this conception acceptable to religion? To answer this question significantly we must consider not mere verbal habits common among theologians, however reputable, but the *values* that can be detected—other than the mere value of familiar or high-sounding words—beneath the use of religious terms like perfect or absolute.

Religious Meaning of Absolute

Why is it religiously significant that God be supposed absolute? The reason is at least suggested by the consideration that absoluteness is requisite for complete reliability. What is relative to conditions may fail us if the conditions happen to be unfavorable. Hence if there is to be anything that *cannot* fail, it must be nonrelative, absolute, in those respects to which "reliability" and "failure" have reference. But it is often not noted that this need not be every respect or aspect from which God's nature can be regarded. For there may be qualities in God whose relativity or variability would be neutral to his reliability. To say of a man that (as human affairs go) his reliability is established refers not to every quality of the man, but only to certain principles exhibited in his otherwise highly variable behavior. We do not mean that if something comes close to his eye he will not blink, or that if he is given bad-tasting food he will enjoy it as much as better fare. We mean that his fixed intention to act according to the requirements of the general welfare will not waver, and that his wisdom and skill in carrying out this aim will be constant. But in all this there is not only no implication that conditions will not have effect upon the man, but the very plain implication that they will have plenty of effect. Skill in one set of circumstances means one form of behavior, in another set another form, and the same is true of the intention to serve the general good. Of course, one may argue that complete fixity of good intention and complete constancy of skill imply every other sort of fixity as well. But this has never yet been definitely shown by careful, explicit reasoning, and anything less is inappropriate in as difficult a subject as we are dealing with. General hunches will not do.

A typically invalid argument in this connection is that unless God surveys at once the whole of time and thus is independent of change, he cannot be relied upon to arrange all events with due regard to their relations to all that has gone before and all that is to come after. This argument either rests on an equivocation or it destroys all religious meaning for the divine reliability. For, if it is meant in any clear sense, it implies that every event has been selected by deity as an element in the best of all possible worlds, the ideal total pattern of all time and all existence. But this ideal pattern includes all acts of sin and the most hideous suffering and catastrophe, all the tragedies of life. And what then becomes of the ideas of human responsibility and choice, and of the notion that some deeds ought not to have taken place? These are only the beginning of the absurdities into which the view thrusts us. To mitigate these absurdities theologians introduce various more or less subtle equivocations. Would they not do better to take a fresh start (as indeed many have done) and admit that we have no good religious reason for positing the notion of providence as an absolute contriving of all events according to a completely detailed plan embracing all time? The religious value of such a notion is more negative than positive. It is the mother of no end of chicanery (see the book of Job for some examples), of much deep feeling of injustice (the poor unfortunate being assured that God has deliberately contrived everything as exactly the best way events could transpire), and of philosophical quagmires of paradox and unmeaning verbiage. The properly constituted man does not want to "rely" upon God to arrange all things, including our decisions, in accordance with a plan of all events which fixes every least detail with reference to every other that ever has happened or ever "is to" happen. How many atheists must have been needlessly produced by insistence upon this arbitrary notion, which after all is invariably softened by qualifications surreptitiously introduced *ad hoc* when certain problems are stressed! We shall see later that the really usable meaning of divine reliability is quite different and is entirely compatible with a profound relativity of God to conditions and to change. For the present, I suggest that all we can assert to have obvious religious value is the faith that God is to be relied upon to do for the world all that ought to be done for it, and with as much survey of the future as there ought to be or as is ideally desirable, leaving for the members of the world community to do for themselves and each other all that they ought to be left to do. We cannot assume that what ought to be done for the world by deity is everything that ought to be done at all, leaving the creatures with nothing to do for themselves and for each other. Nor can we assume that the ideal survey of what for us at least constitutes the future is one which fully defines it in every detail, leaving no open alternatives of possibility. So far from being self-evidently of religious value, these assumptions, viewed in the light of history, seem clearly of extreme disvalue. Yet they are often either asserted, or not unequivocally denied or avoided, in the intemperate insistence upon the total absoluteness of deity.

God as Social

We have also to remember that if there is religious value in the absoluteness of God, as requisite for his reliability, there is equally manifest religious value in another trait which seems unequivocally to imply relativity rather than absoluteness. This is the social or personal nature of God. What is a person if not a being qualified and conditioned by social relations, relations to other persons? And what is God if not the supreme case of personality? Those who deny this have yet to succeed in distinguishing their position from atheism, as Hume pointedly noted. Either God really does love all beings, that is, is related to them by a sympathetic union surpassing any human sympathy, or religion seems a vast fraud. The common query Can the Absolute or Perfect Being be personal or social? should really run In what sense, if any, can a social being be absolute or perfect? For God is conceived socially before he is conceived absolutely or as perfect. God is the highest ruler, judge, benefactor; he knows, loves, and assists man; he has made the world with the design of sharing his bliss with lesser beings. The world is a vast society governed by laws instituted by the divine monarch—the supreme personal power to whom all other persons are subject. These are all, more or less clearly, social conceptions—if you like, metaphors (though aimed, as we shall see, at a literal, intuited meaning) drawn from the social life of man. They constitute the universal, popular meaning of "God," in relation to which descriptions such as "absolute," "perfect," "immutable," "impassive," "simple," and the like, are technical refinements aimed at logical precision. They seek to define the somewhat vague ideas of *highest* ruler, *supreme* power, or *author of all*, himself without author or origin. "Immutable," for example, is an attempted definition of the superiority of deity with respect to death and degeneration, and also with respect to vacillation of will due to fear, or other weakness. Earthly rulers are all brought low by death; and their promises and protection and execution of justice must always be discounted somewhat in anticipation of the effect upon them of changing circumstances and the development of their own motives, the growth of good and evil in their own hearts. God is not under sentence of death, cannot decay; and his convenant abides, nor is his wisdom ever clouded by storms of blind passion, the effects of strong drink or of disease.

The future of theology depends, I suggest, above all upon the answer to this question: can technically precise terms be found which express the supremacy of God, among social beings, without contradicting his social character? To say, on the one hand, that God is love, to continue to use popular religious terms like Lord, divine will, obedience to God, and on the other to speak of an absolute, infinite, immutable, simple, impassive deity, is either a gigantic hoax of priestcraft, or it is done with the belief that the social connotations of the popular language are ultimately in harmony with these descriptions. Merely to speak of the "mysteriousness" of God is not sufficient. If he escapes all the resources of our language and analysis, why be so insistent upon the obviously quite human concepts, absolute, infinite, perfect, immutable? These too are our conceptions, our terms, fragments of the English or Latin languages. Perhaps after all it is not correct to say God is absolute. How shall we know, if the subject is utterly mysterious and beyond our powers?

The Social Nature of Existence

The question Can a supreme being be social? is important not merely because men generally have meant by

God a supreme social being. There are grounds for thinking that the popular religious emphasis is philosophically
sound, that a supreme being must, for rational reasons, be
conceived socially. Human nature is the supreme instance
of nature in general, as known to us (apart from the "nature" of God himself), and moreover, it is the instance
which in some respects at least is much more certainly and
intimately known to us than any other. Human nature is
social through and through. All our thought is some sort of
conversation or dialogue or social transaction; when we
have no one else to converse with, we converse, silently or
even aloud, with ourselves. We love and hate and sympathize, not only in relation to others but in relation to our
own past, future, or potential selves. Not only human beings stimulate such response, but animals, plants, moun-
tains, ships, the moon, colors, sounds (think of groaning
brakes, growling thunder, merry sunshine). One may say
simply, all classes of concrete objects at least can be social
objects for man. What would poetry be without personifi-
cation, overt or implicit; what would art be without em-
pathy, which is social response of a kind?

Now, further, not simply man, but all life whatsoever,
has social structure. All organisms on the multicellular
level are associations of cells. There is scarcely a line between societies and individuals formed by societies which
reach a sufficient grade of integration. Cells themselves are
associations of similar molecules and atoms. It becomes a
question of how broadly one wishes to use terms where one
says that the social begins, if indeed it ever begins, in the
ascending scale of emergence. And the higher one goes in
the scale the more obviously do the social aspects assume a
primary role. Does this point to the conclusion that the
supreme being is not social at all?

There are even more ultimate considerations. Logical

analysis shows, according to such high authorities as Peirce and Whitehead, that the "social" in its most general sense is definable as the synthesis of all the universal categories. It is the union of absolute and relative, independent and dependent, freedom and order, individual and universal, quality and structure, and so on. A nonsocial conception is only arrived at by reducing some category to the zero case. Thus a mere "machine" is what a society would become if the element of routine interdependence should completely suppress the aspect of individual initiative or originality, or if quality (feeling) should vanish, leaving mere structure. And a wholly absolute and hence nonsocial deity is one to which the category of relation—without reference to which even "absolute" has no meaning—is denied application. Thus mechanism, materialism, and absolutism can all be viewed as special cases of the same error, the arbitrary reduction of one or more aspects of sociality to zero. A category so completely ultimate for thought and life as relation (or as felt quality) can, it seems, be assigned null value only in the case of "nonentity." Those who spoke of the wholly absolute deity as the great void perhaps spoke a little more truly than they intended.

The purpose of the foregoing discussion—whose implications could be fully set forth only in a treatise on metaphysics—is not to prove that all things, and therefore even God, must or can be conceived as social in nature; but only to show that the common antithesis between the personal or social deity of religion, and the impersonal or nonsocial supreme being of philosophy, is to be viewed with suspicion. Some of the greatest philosophies, from Plato to Whitehead, have held, with varying degrees of explicitness and consistency, that the social structure is the ultimate structure of all existence; and never has this idea been so explicitly and competently defended as during the last hundred years. Whitehead's supreme conception, for example, is that of a society of actual occasions, related one to another by the sympathetic bond of "feeling of feeling." Peirce's doctrine of agapism was similar. So was Fechner's "daylight view." And Fechner and Whitehead—in some passages, also Peirce—and many other recent thinkers, have held that deity is the supreme case of the social principle, rather than an exception to it.

Social Deity and Creation

It may be thought that a socially conceived God could not be the creator. Can a member of a society create that society? Here we must remember the theological principle of "eminence." God, if social, is eminently or supremely so. On the other hand, that which in the eminent form is called divine creation, in a milder or ordinary form must be exhibited by lesser beings such as man. Man certainly is social. If then ordinary sociality is ordinarily creative, eminent sociality will be eminently creative, divinely creative. And ordinary sociality is, in a humble sense, creative. A man contributes creatively to the concrete actuality of his friends and enemies, and they to his. We *make* each other what we are, in greater or less degree.

The more important members of a society contribute more largely and vitally to the actuality of other members. The supreme member of a society would contribute most vitally and largely to the actuality of all. However, we shall be told, all this is not really "creation," since it presupposes a matter and at most adds a new form. In the first place, no one has proved or can possibly prove (against Peirce, Whitehead, et al.) that there is any "matter," apart from social terms and relations. Electrons and protons are, for all that anyone knows, simply the lowest actual levels of social existence. It may well be that a human mind is not sufficiently important in the world to call an electron into being where none was before. However, we do, by our thoughts and feelings, influence the formation of nerve cells (in the first years of life), and even more, of molecules in the nerves. This is not creation in the eminent sense, but it differs from this only as we might expect the ordinary to differ from the eminent. And the influence of our thought and feeling upon nerve cells and molecules is either a blind mystery, or it is a social influence, as Peirce and Whitehead, and before them (less clearly) Leibnitz, have pointed out.

That the human creator always has a given concrete actuality to work with does not of itself establish a difference between him and God, unless it be admitted as made out that there was a first moment of creation. For if not, then God, too, creates each stage of the world as successor to a preceding phase. Only a dubious interpretation of an obscure parable, the book of Genesis, stands between us and this view. What does distinguish God is that the preceding phase was itself created by God, so that he, unlike us, is never confronted by a world whose coming to be antedates his own entire existence. There is no presupposed "stuff" alien to God's creative work; but rather everything that influences God has already been influenced by him, whereas we are influenced by events of the past with which we had nothing to do. This is one of the many ways in which eminence is to be preserved, without falling into the negations of classical theology.

Analogical Concepts and Metaphysical Uniqueness

It would be a misunderstanding of the social doctrine to accuse it of denying the radical difference between God and nondivine beings. Whitehead (and something similar might be said of Fechner) is so anxious that this difference should not be slurred over that he never, save once in conversation, has described God as a "society of occasions" (with "personal order") because, although that is what, in his system, God must be, it is equally clear that *this* society has a metaphysically unique status and character. By a metaphysically unique status and character I mean one whose distinctiveness can be defined through purely universal categories. It is impossible to define what is unique about my youngest brother in terms of categories alone. And if deity were conceived merely as very superior to man, this description might, for all we could know, apply to myriads of individuals somewhere in the universe. Besides, the description contains a nonmetaphysical term, man. But according to the view presented in this book, a purely metaphysical description applicable only to the one individual, God, is possible. Thus God is the *one individual conceivable a priori*. It is in this sense that concepts applied to him are analogical rather than simply univocal, in comparison to their other applications. For in all other cases, individual otherness is a mere specificity under more general characteristics—thus, my (not wholly definable) nuance of wisdom rather than yours. But in the case of deity, the most general conceptions, without anything more specific, suffice to "individuate" (though not, as we shall see, to particularize or concretize). The old dualities of creating and created, necessary and contingent, perfect and imperfect, expressed this metaphysical or a priori otherness of God. But, as generally stated, they did so in self-contradictory fashion. And it was not seen that, with respect to the category of relation, for example, a metaphysically unique status is definable in another way than through the simple denial of relativity. If the negative "nonrelatedness" is purely categorial, the positive "all-relatedness" is equally so. And we shall find that there is no logical reason why both may not apply to diverse aspects of deity. Then the metaphysical uniqueness would be a double one: no other being, in *any* aspect, could be either wholly relative or wholly nonrelative. Thus, while all beings have some measure of "absoluteness" or independence of relationships and some measure of "relativity," God, and only God, is in one aspect of his being strictly or maximally absolute, and in another aspect no less strictly or maximally relative. So both "relative" and "nonrelative" are analogical, not univocal, in application to deity. And since "social" is, in this reference, equivalent to the synthesis of independent and dependent, social also is analogical in its theological application. Accordingly, our doctrine does not "humanize" or anthropomorphize deity, but preserves a distinction that is completely metaphysical between deity and all else.

The distinction may be expressed under any category. For example, God is the only unconditionally "necessary" existent. What is unconditionally necessary in God, however, is not all of God, though it is unique to him. And in another aspect, God is not only possessed of accidents, but he is the sole being who possesses or could possibly possess all actual accidental being as his own actuality. Other beings are in no aspect strictly necessary, and in no aspect maximally accidental, but always and in all aspects something middling under both categories. In this middling character lies their "imperfection." The mediocre way in which they illustrate categories like possibility, necessity, relativity, independence, is their real otherness to the divine, not the mere fact that they do illustrate this or that category. Tradition put it otherwise, thus: "God is not subject to the category of relation, or of potentiality, or of passivity, etc."

To be sure, there are some apparent qualifications to be made of this historical account. There was said to be relation among the persons of the Trinity; and also God could

be said to have "extrinsic potentiality," since his existence
is the possibility of the world's existence. But these qualifications amount to little. "Relation" here is not the category
of relativity in the basic or primary sense which is in question in this book. For that sense is the ability of a thing to
express in its own nature those other things which, among
alternatively possible or contingent things, happen to exist.
(Persons of the Trinity, of course, are noncontingent.)
This meaning of relation is, as we shall see, the fundamental
one. Without it there could be no knowledge of what contingent things actually exist, and what possibilities of existence are unactualized. Moreover, necessity is a negative
or at least an abstract conception. It may be defined as that
whose nonexistence is not possible; or as that which, being
common to all possibility (its least common denominator,
or abstract identity), has no possible alternative. On the
other hand, Peirce [2] has shown that the definition of the
possible as the nonnecessary presupposes another and positive meaning, that of spontaneous variety, particularity.
Extrinsic potentiality is also, like relation between exclusively necessary factors, a derivative or negative form of
its category. Plato extrinsically "produced" Leibnitz, in
that the actual coming to be of Leibnitz did not change or
enrich the actuality of Plato. He who causes others to
reach the promised land but himself remains outside—as
the historical Plato remained outside the philosophy of
Leibnitz (in the sense that he did not know or enjoy it)—
exercises extrinsic potency, potency of producing but not
of being. Alternative possible effects of such an agent cannot be regarded as deliberate deeds on his part. To decide
this, when deciding that was possible, is to be in one state
of decision when another was possible. In so far as Plato

2. See, in *Collected Papers,* especially Vols. I and VI, discussions of
firstness, possibility, chance, variety, spontaneity.

consciously chose the kind of successors he was to have,
just so far his potency was intrinsic as well as extrinsic.
And he was a human being, able to produce a human being's characteristic effects, only because he did exercise
intrinsic potency. Conscious freedom is decision among alternative possibilities of intrinsic being. Plato chose the
sort of influence he was to have by choosing what he was
himself to be. This is all that can be meant by conscious
choice. It may be that God has only to say, "Let there be
light," and there is light. But God's saying "Let there be
light" is a state of his being, and a nonnecessary state, for
otherwise either we have a vicious regress, the "Let there
be light" becoming something outside himself, so that he
must have said Let such a saying be; or else the saying is
his very essence, and then he could not possibly have failed
to say "Let there be light," and the saying can have been
no decision, no free act at all.

Critique of the Negative Theology

That God can be individually designated by the categories, not only in negative but in positive application, not
only by nonrelativity but by supreme relativity, reveals the
falsity of the familiar idea that these categories are merely
human or creaturely affairs. For whereas creatures exhibit
the categories only in a nondistinctive fashion, one creature being relative (for example) in the same categorical
manner as another, and thus sharing the category with that
other, God is relative in a categorically unique manner,
which is shared with nothing else. What can this mean, if
not that the referent of the category is something original
with God, in some fashion God himself? Other creatures
participate in being as expressed in the category; God *is*
that being—as tradition had it, with the sole difference

that tradition mistakenly reasoned as though only in their negative application were categories unique to God. This mistake led to the metaphysical false modesty of seeking to honor deity by refusing to apply any of our positive conceptions to him. If a man who says yes is still mere man, does a man who says no thereby transcend humanity and understand the divine nature? At least—the negative theologian may reply—he will not misunderstand it. We must object as follows. A man will not misunderstand an entity if he does not think about it at all. What is the difference between refraining from applying any concept to a thing and just not thinking about it? If, then, the negative theologian is really thinking, he must be doing something more than merely refusing to apply human concepts to deity. He must actually be applying human, albeit negative, conceptions. He is asserting that whatever "dependence," "potentiality," "change," may refer to, there is none of it in deity. How can he know this unless he understands something positive in deity which is incompatible with such categories? And my contention is that the absoluteness, for example, which we have reason to attribute to deity is not only compatible with, but requires, a unique relativity, as another aspect of the same divine being.

The inadequacy of the negative theology comes close to the obvious when we are told that God is not really "good" but only, not nongood. Thus a double negative is made distinct from a positive. In three-valued logics a double negative is indeed distinguished from a positive, but only because of the third value of "indeterminate" as between positive and negative. This third value is not something superior to the other two values, but only something potential or ambiguous with respect to them. The negative theology thus could only mean that God's goodness or non-goodness is something undecided, or ambiguous. Is that what religions mean to asert in their praise of him?

Literalness of Theism

When Charles Wesley, who must have known something of religious values, wrote: "Father, thou art all compassion, Pure unbounded love thou art," he was not distinguishing God by denying relativity or passivity to him. Yet he was distinguishing God metaphysically. For all other beings limit their compassion at some point. They are sympathetic, passive, relative, in some directions, not in all. Their love is not pure, but mixed with indifference, hardness of heart, resistance to or incapacity for some relativities. We do not "love" literally, but with qualifications, and metaphorically. Love, defined as social awareness, taken literally, is God. It is much more true that we are socially unaware than that we are socially aware, and this by an infinite ratio. God is socially aware—period. Thus he is the literal instance (because the original one) of the categories; they are himself in his individual essence, though not, as we shall see, in his total actuality. It is by self-flattery that we imagine we exemplify the category, say, of "knowledge" *simpliciter*. We guess, we have probable opinions, we unclearly feel, but know . . . ? It is God who knows. Why then the negative theology? Our own natures it is which (partially) negate the categories, not God's.

Perhaps I am overlooking needed qualifications, but to me it seems that theology (so far as it is the theory of the essence of deity) is the most literal of all sciences of existence. It is anthropology (including theological anthropology) that is shot full of metaphors and statements never literally true. We like to think we are wise and our enemies foolish, but always we are also foolish and our enemies also

wise. Man is never quite what he says that he is. Only of
God is he privileged to affirm the naked truth—if he takes
care and does not fall down and worship some theological
tradition which has crystallized theological thought pre-
maturely. Thus God is wise—period. He is unborn—period.
He is everlasting—period. He is socially aware of all beings, the actual as actual, the possible as possible—period.
True, one might say, man is born—period. He is neither
wholly wise nor wholly foolish—period. But these statements are full of vagueness, and do not distinguish man
from elephants and innumerable other creatures. One might
also say that the pure wisdom of deity has been interpreted
in at least two basically different ways, as a *totum simul*
of all time, and as an intuition of all events down to the
present, with perpetual addition of new events as they occur. And unborn might mean, with no quality that has come
into being; or it might mean, with an individual essence
that is, without ever having become, yet with accidents that
have become. But this issue is definite, and whichever way
it is correctly decided we have a literal statement which may
be literally true, and would not be true of any individual
other than God. Traditional theology somewhat oversimpli-
fied, in its literal statements, and in its theory of the superior safety of negative propositions; and then it tried to
atone for this by indulging in various metaphors, such as
the service of God or the overflowing of the divine goodness
or the divinity of Jesus.

No doubt in religion, as distinct from theology, or in theological anthropology, as distinct from the mere theory of
the divine essence, metaphors are called for, in order to
move the imaginations and hearts of men. But the pure
theory of divinity is literal, or it is a scandal, neither poetry
nor science, neither well reasoned nor honestly dispensing
with reasoning. It is precisely the being with a necessary

essence that, as such, must be definable a priori. The contingent is that which transcends reason, and can ultimately only be felt as sheer fact. It is not in pure theology that the "symbolic" nature of expression reaches its climax but in history and sociology. Who knows literally what "romanticism" or "liberalism" or "revolution" or "social patterns" or "tyranny" or "free enterprise" or "freedom of speech" may be? Not that these ideas are invalid or unimportant, but that they are bound to be less precise than theological terms ought to be and can be.

If someone should say that I have been using "literal" and "metaphorical" in an unusual, nonliteral, and even metaphorical sense, I should reply that I have apprehensions this may perhaps be true. I should be happy to be taught how to put the matter more precisely.

If theological truth can be conveyed in comparatively simple literal statements, why, it may be asked, must long books be written on the subject? There are at least two reasons. The one is simply—history. Theologies have grown, and errors are beloved along with the truth in the seemingly unitary beauty of the great traditions, in which literal truths, literal errors, and charming but equivocal metaphors are blended. Perhaps it is useless to reason at length with such traditional prejudices, but I feel impelled to do so. The other reason is that theological terms, though literal, derive this literal meaning from intuitions which are not conspicuous in normal human experience, and must be carefully distinguished from other, more conspicuous intuitions with which they may be confused. What we need, one might say, is not metaphors to convey the meaning, but the thorough elimination of the metaphorical meanings which are always threatening to substitute themselves; thus the notions of God as judge or as monarch are highly and dangerously metaphorical. So is the notion of the human soul as one entity from birth to death, a subtle something within the body and not identical with the experiences and feelings or with any phenomenal unity of these. The notion of cause as completely determining its effects is a metaphorical confusion of logical consequence with temporal sequence, or of clay molding with process as such, and the like. These are not the directly intuited categorical features, aspects of God's very being, which are at issue in theology. The positivistic doctrine of physicalism is a systematic metaphor which would apparently deprive us of ever speaking literally of anything but "chronogeometrical" structures. It is not true that the psychical must be referred to indirectly. Suffering, joy, memory, hope, mean their referents directly. And so far as "soul" is not meant directly, it is, I believe, legend, or poetic embellishment on what is meant directly, namely, the continuity of personal experience—so far as it is continuous. That "substance" is metaphor everyone knows. Thus it is philosophy that is metaphorical, and it can become literal, I am convinced, only when it is willing to accept a literal theism, which will avoid the oversimplifications, compensated by metaphor, of traditional theologies as well as of atheism and positivism. Just as giving up what is metaphorical in "substance" or in "cause" does not mean giving up the human person, or the essential interconnectedness of process, so it need not, and I think could not, mean giving up the divine person and the divine influence promotive of a measure of world order.

Once more, "divine person" is not meant metaphorically. It is the human being that more or less exhibits personal continuity and integrity, God that literally is always the same personal "I." An animal, which cannot say God, equally cannot say I. There is no derivation of the first notion from the second; but the two are from the outset in contrast in experience. The animal feels both itself and God (for reasons to be seen in Chapter III) and thinks neither; we feel and can think both. We are, indeed, likely to call the divine "I," "Truth" or "reality"; that is, we think of certain abstract aspects of the inclusive something, and do not quite realize consciously that it must be an inclusive experience, the model of all experiences in its personal unity. If the foregoing is incorrect (and my saying it is no proof of its correctness) then so far as I can see the idea of God is meaningless. The question, is there a God, for me at least coincides with the question, can God be directly and literally known (in individual essence, though not in actuality or in concrete fullness)? This book seeks not to answer but to analyze the question.

In What Sense God Is Unknowable

We must guard against a further misunderstanding. To say that the categories suffice to designate the divine individual is infinitely far from implying that the entire actuality of deity is humanly knowable. It is one thing to know an individual as distinguished from all others. It is another to know that same individual in its actual "state," as distinguished from other states possible for it, though impossible for any other individual. Traditional doctrine rejected the notion of alternative possible states for the divine individual. But if God is supremely relative as well as supremely nonrelative, then in his relative aspect his actuality varies with variations in the things to which he is relative and is potential with respect to potential terms of his relativity. To know the actuality of deity, as relative to the present and past actual universe, would be to know that universe as God knows it. But in fact we do not know exactly and distinctly even a single concrete item of that universe. Unless it can be proved that the number of items is finite, our knowledge of the relative actuality of God must be set down as infinitesimal. Even if the number of items be finite, since our grasp of any one item is more or less vague or uncertain, it seems that no finite ratio could express the deficiency of our awareness of the universe, and of God as relative to the universe. Once more we see the ineptness of the notion: the creatures we know, God is hidden from us. The creatures as they are coincide with the creatures as terms of divine cognitive relations. To have knowledge of the creatures as they are is in so far to know as God knows. Adding self-knowledge, we should have knowledge of the divine way of knowing. Alas, it is the creatures, and hence God as relative to them, that escape forever our apprehension. That he has relations we can know, but just what relations to just what, we can never precisely know in even a single concrete case. Why indeed should our ability to understand the divine art product surpass our ability to understand the divine artist? Is not the work a phase of the life of the worker?

True enough, God is not "subject" to the categories, as though they were something antecedent to his own individuality. As we have suggested, in the form in which they apply to him, the categories are that individuality.

Religious Meaning of Perfection

We have been considering the philosophical or methodological importance of the uniqueness of deity. Let us now consider more closely its religious import. As we have seen, the religious value of the term absolute is that it connotes reliability or stability. What, then, is the religious significance enshrined in the idea of metaphysically unique excellence or perfection? At least part of it is clearly this, that whereas, in all other cases, admiration, respect, reverence, for anyone or anything, become inappropriate if carried beyond a certain point, here, and here only, we are free to admire and respect and love without limit. Unlimited admiration for anything other than God is idolatry; but unlimited admiration for God is true piety. If, however, we were forced to admit that even God must be admired grudgingly, then idolatry would lose its distinctive meaning. It scarcely needs argument that there is religious value in the contrast between idolatry and piety, and that the term perfect, whatever else it may connote, is felt to refer to that in God which justifies this contrast. I think, also, it is sound intuition that leads people to resist doctrines which seem to imply that there can be no piety free from idolatry since, according to these doctrines, no being is worthy of unqualified respect.

Complete Independence not Admirable

But, supposing that God is to be conceived worthy of utter respect, and in that sense "perfect," it may not follow that God is quite everything that has customarily been associated with this adjective. For it is entirely possible that theologians have sometimes respected things which, when more carefully considered, are seen not to be suitable objects of this respect. The being in the highest degree admirable will have, in the highest degree or manner, all properties that deserve admiration. But even tyrants and scoundrels have actually been admired and, it rather seems, admired sometimes for their very tyranny and rascality. To some of us, nothing is more deeply shocking than certain directions frequently taken by theological admiration. What is the ideal of the tyrant? Is it not that, while the fortunes of all should depend upon the tyrant's will, he should depend as little as possible, ideally not at all, upon the wills and fortunes of others? This one-sided independence, in ideally complete or "absolute" form, was held the

crowning glory of deity! Sheer independence in every respect whatsoever, while all else in every respect depended
upon him, was regarded as essential to God's perfection.
There are those, including Berdyaev and many other good
and wise men, who find no stimulus to admiration or respect
in this doctrine.

Of course there are modes of independence which are
admirable. But is it any less true that there are modes of
dependence which we all admire, and of independence which
we detest? The father that as little as possible depends
upon the will and welfare of his child is an inhuman monster.
Let the child—say, a daughter—be happy, let her be
miserable, let her deeply desire this or deeply detest that,
let her develop in a moral or in a vicious direction, it is all
one to the independent parent, who goes his way in complete neutrality to all such alternatives (this neutrality
being the exact meaning of absoluteness or independence)
wholly uninfluenced by weal or woe, love or hate, preference
or detestation, in the unlucky child that, in such a one-
sided way, depends upon the parent. Is this really an ideal?
Is not the correct ideal rather this, that the parent should
be influenced in appropriate, and only in appropriate,
ways by the child's desires and fortunes? One should not
simply agree to every whim of the child, or strive always
to save her from pain or furnish her with pleasure. Nor
should one be sunk in misery with her every sorrow, or
fantastically elated with her every triumph. But neither
should one try to act and think and feel just as one would
have acted or thought or felt had the child's joy been sorrow, or her sorrow joy, or her likes dislikes. Yet God, we
are told, is impassive and immutable and without accidents,
is just as he would be in his action and knowledge and being
had we never existed, or had all our experiences been otherwise. Instead of attributing to God an eminently appro-

priate dependence upon us, the majority of theologians simply denied dependence of any and every sort. This seems plainly an idealization of the tyrant-subject relationship, as Whitehead, a critic as fair and moderate as he is profound, has reminded us.

The Independence Which Is Admirable

Suppose a man says, I can be a good man, do my duty, only so long as a certain friend continues to live and to encourage me. Our feeling will surely be that, while it is natural and human to lean upon friends for moral assistance, still a man should do his duty whatever anyone else may do. In ethical character one should be as independent as possible of other contingent beings. Thus to depend for doing one's duty upon others is inappropriate, unadmirable dependence. God then, as object of piety, will be in highest degree, or utterly, independent of our actions and fortunes for the preservation of his holiness of will. That is, he will promote the highest cosmic good, come what may. But it does not in the least follow that what God will do to promote the cosmic good will be uninfluenced by our actions and fortunes, or that how he will think and feel about the world will in no way reflect what is going on in the world. The man who does his duty regardless of what happens will not have the same specific duties regardless of what happens. And with different duties he will perform different acts with different specific intentions, ideas, and feelings.

Suppose, on the other hand, a man says, I can be equally happy and serene and joyous regardless of how men and women suffer around me. Shall we admire this alleged independence? I think not. Why should we admire it when it is alleged of God? I have yet to learn a good answer to this question. On the other hand, if we see a person who is dragged down into helpless misery by the sight of suffering in others, we feel that this response is as inappropriate as the opposite one of gay serenity would be in the same circumstances. And there is no inconsistency in condemning both responses, for a clear logical principle can be applied to both. This is that we should respond to the total situation appropriately, not just to a part of it, or inappropriately. The suffering of the world is not the world; there is also the joy of the world. If the one should sadden us, the other should delight us. He who refuses to rejoice with the joy of others is as selfish as he who refuses to grieve with their sorrows. Indeed, as has been often remarked, it is if anything a rarer unselfishness to be really inspired by the happiness of our friends than to be saddened by their unhappiness. For the happiness of others may inspire us with envy instead of sympathetic pleasure. Such neutralization by envy of sympathetic dependence for our own happiness upon that of others is scarcely admirable!

Proportional Dependence

The notion that total emotional independence is admirable seems, then, to be without foundation in experience. There *is* an admirable independence, but it is independence in basic ethical purpose, not in specific concrete experience and happiness. There is also admirable dependence, which is appropriate response, duly proportionate to the balance of factors in the world known to us, of sympathetic rejoicing and sorrowing. Why not attribute to the divine response the ideal of such appropriateness, or proportionality, of dependence? The requirement of piety seems entirely compatible with such attribution.

To depend upon others emotionally through sympathy is to change when they change—for example, to grow in joy when they do. But if God changes, it is often argued, then he changes either for the worse or for the better. If the former, how can we admire him without stint? If the latter, then it seems he must previously have lacked something, and been incomplete and imperfect. The first horn of the dilemma need not concern us, unless it can be proved that there is ever more sorrow than joy in the world. For if there is always more satisfaction than dissatisfaction, then God should always have more reason to rejoice than to grieve over the world, and since he can retain the consciousness of past joys, there will always be a *net increment* of value accruing to God at each moment. Now if life were not more satisfying than otherwise, could it go on? Is there anything to maintain the will to live save satisfaction in living? I do not see that there is. Hence I shall confine my attention to the second horn of the dilemma, that a God who increases in value must previously have lacked some value, and therefore have been imperfect. My reply is that, as we are here using the term, perfect means completely worthy of admiration and respect, and so the question becomes, is such complete admirableness infringed by the possibility of enrichment in total value? I say it is not. We do not admire a man less because we know he would be a happier man if his son, who is wretched, became well and happy, or because we anticipate that when a child is born to him it will enrich his life with many new joys. Admiration is not directed to happiness, except so far as we feel that a person does or does not attain the happiness appropriate to the state of the world as known to him. We admire not the amount but the appropriateness of the joy. We rejoice in another's happiness, we grieve over his misfortune, but we do not praise or blame or admire on this account, unless we think the good or bad fortune is the person's own doing. So far as it is due rather to the decisions of others, which were their responsibility, not his, then it determines not our respect, but only the tone of our sympathy or participatory feeling, toward the person. Why should it be otherwise in relation to God? If God rejoices less today than he will tomorrow, but ideally appropriately at both times, our reverence for him should in no way be affected by the increase in joy. Indeed, if he were incapable of responding to a better world with greater satisfaction, this should infringe upon our respect; for it would imply a lack of proportionality in the divine awareness of things.

Gratitude is the appropriate expression of genuine indebtedness, of really having received benefit from others. Conceited men would perhaps like to avoid occasions for gratitude, so that they might boast of their independence. But no good man blessed with a beloved wife is sorry to feel that without her he could not have been so happy. To God each of us is dearer than wife to husband, for no human being knows the inner experiences of another human being so intimately as they are known to God. And to know experiences is to appreciate them; for the value of experience is just the experience itself. As we are indebted to a few persons for the privilege of feeling something of the quality of their experiences, so God is indebted to *all* persons for the much fuller enjoyment of the same privilege. God is not conceited or envious; therefore he has no motive for wishing to escape or deny this indebtedness. It is envious men, priests, theologians, guardians—in some cases one could almost say watchdogs—of the divine majesty, who attribute such an attitude, such unbridled will to independence, to God. (No doubt God's sense of indebtedness to us lacks some of the connotations of "gratitude," such as the sense of a common moral frailty, almost miraculously overcome in a certain case.)

Sympathetic Dependence

I have been contending that there are appropriate forms of dependence, in relation to certain terms. To this an opponent may object that the appropriateness is not determined solely by the nature of the entities toward which the dependence obtains, but involves also the nature of that which is thus made dependent. It is appropriate for man to depend upon man, not for the supreme being to depend upon anything. But my proposition is that the higher the being the more dependence of certain kinds will be appropriate for it. One does not expect an oyster to depend for its joy or sorrow upon my joy or sorrow, as such, or even upon that of other oysters to any great extent. Sympathetic dependence is a sign of excellence and waxes with every ascent in the scale of being. Joy calls for sympathetic joy, sorrow for sympathetic sorrow, as the most excellent possible forms of response to these states. The eminent form of sympathetic dependence can only apply to deity, for this form cannot be less than an omniscient sympathy, which depends upon and is exactly colored by every nuance of joy or sorrow anywhere in the world. It would certainly not be appropriate for man to even try to sympathize with all life. How could he hope to do such a thing? Thus I grant to the opponent that what is "appropriate dependence" varies with the subject as well as the object of the dependence relation. But I deny that zero dependence for happiness is ever appropriate, and I assert that the closest to such zero dependence would occur at the bottom, not the top of the scale of beings, while the top, the most eminent form of dependence for happiness, would be maximal dependence, dependence upon all life even to its least nuance for the exact happiness of the eminent individual.

I invite you to perform with me a mental experiment.

Imagine someone to read aloud an eloquent poem, in the presence of: (A) a glass of water, (B) an ant, (C) a dog, (D) a human being unacquainted with the language of the poem, (E) a human being knowing the language but insensitive to poetry, (F) a person sensitive to poetry and familiar with the language. Now I submit that each member of this series is superior, in terms of the data, to its predecessors, and that each is more, not less, dependent upon or relative to the poem as such, including its meanings as well as its mere sounds. The molecules of water will be utterly "impassible" (the theological term) to the words of the poem as words, and not even much affected by the mere physical sounds. The ant, since it has hearing, will be affected by the physical sounds more drastically, it seems probable, than the water. The dog will not only hear and be influenced by the sound, as such, but will have some sense of the emotional tones of voice, and may be quite excited by these. It may also have a feeling of familiarity concerning some of the words. The human being not knowing the language will receive more varied influences of this kind and will enjoy some sense of the verbal music of the poem, which may furnish a rather absorbing experience. The insensitive, but comprehending, listener will be given a variety of images and ideas, even though without intense esthetic feeling or adequate integration. The adequate listener may go through a deep and thousandfold adventure of thought and feeling. Thus we see that the simple correlation of inferior with dependent or relative is anything but a report upon experience. The identification of "absolute" and "supreme" has to be proved, not blandly assumed, and it is in the teeth of the experiences without which we could not know what either absolute or supreme could reasonably mean.

The Metaphysics of Democracy

It would be easy to multiply illustrations all tending to show the baselessness of the assumption that the best or optimal dependence is zero dependence. I dare affirm that this assumption is a blunder so great—and so influential—that one might scarcely hope in the whole history of thought to find a greater or more influential. And this unwarranted assumption, this metaphysical snobbery toward relativity, dependence, or passivity, toward responsiveness or sensitivity, this almost slavish (doubtless it would be too much to say knavish) worship of mere absoluteness, independence, and one-sided activity or power, this transcendentalized admiration of politico-ecclesiastical tyranny, the ideal of which is to act on all while avoiding reaction from them, this spiritual blindness and false report upon experience is, as we are about to see, the chief source of the metaphysico-theological paradoxes of which so much has been heard. Just as the loyal Roman Catholic (and, according to official statements, everyone in an overwhelmingly Catholic State), unless high in the hierarchy, can have little hope either of influencing or of evading papal decrees, so, and in a more strict sense, there is, according to the old theology, no hope either of influencing or of evading divine decrees. The politically, and I am confident theologically, sounder principle is rather this, that he who is most adequately influenced by all may most appropriately exert influence upon all. The best ruler is an intermediary in the universal interaction, able to moderate and harmonize actions because all that is done is done also to him, whose reaction to this action absorbs and transmutes all influences into a counterinfluence, integrative and harmonizing in tendency, discouraging excessive factors and encouraging insufficient ones. This is the democratic idea of rule, and it is an ideal of equality only by virtue of the fact that men are essentially of one species in their capacity to absorb influences, therefore in their right to exert power. The king, be he the best of men, is only too largely independent, insensitive, ignorant, apathetic, nonrelative, toward what goes on in the hearts of men, or even in their kitchens, and it is therefore that he cannot be trusted with supreme power over men. But if there be a being supreme in sensitivity, in nonapathy, in cognitive relativity, then no man who understands what he is doing will wish to deny this being supreme power, least of all on the basis of the democratic principle. For to say God is supremely sensitive is to say that in his rule he allots to us a privilege of participation in governing which goes infinitely beyond a mere ballot. It means that with every decision, however secret, that takes place in our minds we are casting a vote which will surely be taken account of and will surely produce effects in the divine decisions. More of this in the third chapter.

Skeptics Who Argue from a Medieval Premise

It seems needful to remark, however disagreeably, that it is playing the game of medieval theology to argue, even to an atheistic or positivistic conclusion, from the assumed identification of the question, is there a supreme being, a being whose superiority or admirableness entitles him to the name of God, with the question, very different, as I am suggesting, is there a being wholly absolute, independent, nonrelative. He who reasons from this identification is accepting from medieval copy books one of their most arbitrary and pernicious maxims. In this denunciation, I am not quarrelling with straw men. For example, Nicolai Hartmann, in his widely read *Ethics* (III, 266; German ed., p. 740), argues against the idea of God on the ground that if there is a divine purpose our decisions count for nothing. True enough—if the divine purpose is wholly nonrelative to those decisions, if its superiority involves all-round independence! Not true at all—if the superiority actually consists, as spiritual experience implies it must, in a unique relativity to all other beings and their decisions! Is it not time for those who profess no allegiance to medieval doctrines or institutions to cease their unconscious obeisance to the basic medieval postulate? Upon the unjustified prejudice, the rotten foundation, of the worship of mere power or absoluteness, we ought to build no edifice, sacred or profane. He who speaks, *even to attack it*, of the idea of a radically superior or excellent being ought, if he is honest, to mean by excellent what he himself, upon most careful reflection, self-examination, and discussion with those he deems wise and good, feels to be excellent. Or else he ought to make it quite clear that he is discussing not the question Is there a being capable of arousing in wise and good men, so far as aware of him, that unstinted admiration and respect which is worship or reverence?—that is to say, the question Is there a God?—but the different question Is there a being which, unworthy of such reverence, might yet (so far as it could exist or be believed to exist) receive it from those men whose sense of values (at least, as expressed in their theories) is confused or one-sided? The atheism which attacks ecclesiasticism by assuming the latter's scale of values may be excusable as a political counterbalance, but what has it to do with rational inquiry purporting to investigate the nature of existence? Yet I know of comparatively little discussion of the theistic question, pro or con, that is not marred by this prejudicial procedure. Happily, current practice shows considerable improvement in this regard.

Perhaps I have been too frank—even uncharitable. Of course there are many counterbalancing factors in orthodox churches, thanks to which many of their members may, not only in their lives but in most of their thinking about God, express a nobler ideal than many of the rest of us. Yet the abstract principle I have referred to is not, to my understanding, reasonably to be credited with this result. And for the benefit of any who may not be fully aware of what has been happening in non-Roman theological circles it may need to be said that the judgment I have been expressing can appeal to a number of precedents in distinguished theological works of recent times. My own father, over fifty years ago, encountered and accepted similar teaching when he attended divinity school. Yet the youngest critics of theism (though much less often than formerly) may still sometimes be seen trying to deal with the question of deity as though it were admitted on all hands that whatever God may be he cannot be genuinely relative or passive to influence. And the latest defenders of scholasticism, as I have some reason to know, generally refuse to bestow any but the most crudely inaccurate and careless expressions of contempt upon the notion of God as the supremely relative being. It is hard to make headway against both the orthodox and most of their fashionable opponents! And it is distressing to see that what brings these groups together in this matter is the very tenet that embodies in metaphysical form the cause of much of the disgust of the latter group with the former, namely, its false scale of values or notion of excellence.

I have, to be sure, been told by a learned scholar (not, of course, for the first time) that my interpretation of the great theologians of the past is one-sided, that (for example, in doctrines of the Holy Spirit) they affirmed the divine relativity. So much the better! However, my critic conceded to me that a consistent philosophical analysis of such relativity is not to be credited to any unless quite recent theologies or philosophies.

Anselm and Coe on Divine Compassion

There is a passage in Anselm which seems unwittingly to testify against the doctrine which the great Bishop seeks to expound. Addressing the deity, Anselm reasons thus:

If thou art passionless [i.e., nonrelative, independent], thou dost not feel sympathy; and if thou dost not feel sympathy, thy heart is not wretched from sympathy for the wretched; but this it is to be compassionate. But if thou art not compassionate, whence cometh so great consolation to the wretched? . . .

Truly, thou art compassionate in terms of our experience, but thou art not so in terms of thine own. For, when thou beholdest us in our wretchedness, we experience the effect of compassion, but thou dost not experience the feeling. Therefore, thou art both compassionate, because thou dost save the wretched, and spare those who sin against thee; and not compassionate, because thou art affected by no sympathy for wretchedness. [*Proslogium,* Chap. viii.] [2a]

What does Anselm's statement amount to? Is it not this, that we should love God, not as we love our friends, sympathetically and with appreciation of their sympathy for us, but solely in terms of the benefits which we receive from him—just as crassly utilitarian persons see in friendship only utility? To such a person we should say that the greatest utility of all is the sense of mutual enrichment through sympathetic sharing of feelings and ideas. Anselm's God can give us everything, everything except the right to believe that there is one who, with infinitely subtle and appropriate sensitivity, rejoices in all our joys and sorrows in all our sorrows. But this benefit which Anselm will not

2a. Trans. by S. N. Deane (La Salle, Ill., Open Court Publishing Company, 1945), pp. 13–14.

allow God to bestow upon us is the supreme benefit which
God and only God could give us. We are left with the crude
and blundering sympathies of men, or the alleged sympathies of angels—who, if they exist, are still necessarily
limited in their sensitivity—as the best social responses we
are privileged to occasion. To say, "all the effects of compassion, only not the compassion itself," is to mock us. For
the supreme effect of compassion is to give us the awareness that someone really and literally responds to our feelings with sympathetic appreciation. If God permits us
every privilege, but not that of enriching his life by contributing the unique quality of our own experience to the
more inclusive quality of his, by virtue of his sympathetic
interest in us, then he does less for us than the poorest of
human creatures. What we ask above all is the chance to
contribute to the being of others. This ultimate generosity
of aspiration is stifled by the doctrine that in the supreme
relation in which we stand it is only ourselves, not the other,
that has anything to receive from the relation. "To love,"
it has been said, "is to wish to give rather than to receive";
but in loving God we are, according to Anselm and thousands of other orthodox divines, forbidden to seek to give;
for God, they say, is a totally impassive, nonreceptive, nonrelative being. Such guardians of the divine majesty in my
judgment know not what they do.

The renunciation of genuinely social relations with God
is not the only price paid for maintaining the pure absoluteness of deity. Anselm speaks of God "beholding our wretchedness," but beholding, too, is a passive and relational state.
He should say, God "knows" our sorrow, speaking in terms
of our experience, but not in terms of his own ("experience"?). It is *as if* he knew that we sorrow, but really he
does not; for such knowledge could only be a relation. In
addition, what does it mean to know what sorrow is, but

never to have sorrowed, never to have felt the quality of suffering? I find nothing in my experience that gives meaning to this set of words.

A more recent writer than Anselm, without his feeling of the necessity of theoretical orthodoxy, puts the matter as follows: "The act of worship . . . requires for its highest perfection some conception or sense of compassion felt by God toward his worshipper." [3]

Dare we include God himself in the social whole which it is our mission to live for? We may well be modest when we try to think God's thought concerning himself, and yet we but apply Jesus' own teachings when we say that the love of God toward men, and his desire for love in return, indicate some sort of solidarity of life. Here let us . . . pause, pushing back the speculative questions that press upon us, threatening to fill with curiosity a mind that needs inspiration. Let us hold fast to the thought that individualism no more expresses the life of God than it describes the real life of men. God, as well as men, is a social being . . . He is in earnest when he enters into social relations with us creatures. These relations go to the center of his being, as they go to the center of ours. [4]

One notes that Coe refuses to go into the logical difficulties. As a profound student of religious psychology (along with many other such students) he sees and reports the need for a social conception of deity; but he suggests we should not be too pretentious in seeking to achieve this conception. He does not try to define the sense in which the supreme social being is perfect or independent or absolute. This seems to me preferable to the orthodox proce-

3. George A. Coe, *The Spiritual Life* (New York, Eaton & Mains, 1900), p. 241.
4. Coe, *Religion of a Mature Mind* (Chicago, New York, Toronto, Fleming H. Revell Company, 1902), pp. 184 f.

dure of undertaking the definitions and offering as result
pronouncements which are either meaningless or self-
contradictory, and certainly are not faithful to the religious meanings they claim to interpret. Coe shows effectively how the worship of the Virgin mother had to become
an inadequate and misleading substitute for a truly social
conception of God.

As further evidence of the technical failure of medieval
theology to solve the problem of absoluteness, consider the
following modern summary of the state of the problem
in scholastic circles:

All should admit that the Creator enters into *what are conceived as relations* [italics Rickaby's] to his creatures; and
if many theologians refuse to call these relations *real*, it is
only to save the appearance [*sic*] of asserting any intrinsic
change within the immutable God, or any real dependency.
Others, with the proviso, that the Divine attributes are to be
kept inviolate, say that the relation may be called real, in
order to signify that creation on the part of God is most
really his work, though he does not work after our way of
passing from potency to act and of depending on materials.[5]

It seems almost cruel to comment on this testimony to the
failure of a metaphysical tradition. For it comes to this:
An admittedly disastrous flat denial that God possesses
relation to the creatures is avoided only on the following
condition: that being related to contingent items, items
that might not have been, should itself be a wholly noncontingent relationship! Thus relation-to-Y is to be unconditionally necessary, though its constituent Y is not!
Again, relation-to-Y (not in some, but in all, its properties,
for God knows all) is to be immutable, though Y is not;

5. John Rickaby, *General Metaphysics,* Catholic Manuals of Philosophy
(London, Longmans, Green & Co., 1890), p. 197.

a whole is to be in all respects unchanging, though one of its constituents alters. That logical laws do not allow this is blandly passed over. To assert something while avoiding the "appearance" of asserting its implied consequences is no doubt a common way of philosophizing; but is it too much to ask that after so many centuries of this theological tradition its proponents should stand up and tell us, not what they are willing to appear to assert, but what (free from self-contradiction) they do assert? [6]

Relativity and the Value of Life

Among the many unfortunate implications of the denial of divine relativity are those pertinent to the question: What is the inclusive value of human life? Is it human welfare only? Is it the "glorification" of God defined as so completely absolute that it must be beyond our power to contribute to his greatness? A new era in religion may be predicted as soon as men grasp the idea that it is just as true that God is the supreme beneficiary or *recipient* of achievement, hence supremely relative to all achieved actualities, as that he is the supreme benefactor or *source* of achievement, and in so far nonrelative to its results. There has been a secret poison long working in religious thought and feeling, the poison of man's wanting to be an ultimate recipient of value. Religion then becomes man's self-service, not genuinely his service of God. For if God can be indebted to no one, can receive value from no one, then to speak of serving him is to indulge in equivocation. Really it must, on that assumption, be only the creature who is to be served or benefited. God would be the cause and protector of value; but the value caused and protected must

6. Anyone who believes this can be done might be interested in Father Meehan's controversy with me, in *Journal of Religion*, XXVI (1946), 50–57.

be simply ours. On this time-hallowed view, God was the
mine and the miner from and by which the wealth was dug;
but the ultimate consumer was ourselves.[7] God was the
policeman and judge and ruler, but man was the citizen,
for whose sake the commonwealth existed. It is time that
we consider the possibility that it may be just as blasphemous to suppose ourselves the ultimate recipients, as the
ultimate makers, of achieved good. We are intermediate
and secondary makers of value, intermediate benefactors;
are we not likewise intermediate and secondary recipients
of value, intermediate beneficiaries? The supreme source,
and as well the supreme result, of the entire process of
value-making is, I suggest, the divine life, in its originative
and its consummatory phases, and these phases are genuinely distinct. How this is possible we shall see more clearly
in the following chapters.

7. It is one of my difficulties with H. N. Wieman's theology that for him
achieved good is enjoyed only by creatures, not by God. Yet he says some
very important things about the human attitudes and activities that aid
the achievement. See his *The Source of Human Good* (The University of
Chicago Press, 1946).

CHAPTER II

God as Absolute, Yet Related to All

I T WAS pointed out in the first chapter that "there is an absolute" implies "there are external relations." It was also remarked that the promising medieval beginning of a theory of external relations was vitiated by an illogical reversal or interchange of roles, with respect to such relations as knowing and loving, which, normally internal (at least in ideal), were said to be wholly external to God. We saw, too, that this anomalous reversal in the case of divine relations was entirely owing to the assumption *that relativity as such is a deficiency* and therefore cannot be present in God, the supremely excellent being. Finally, we saw that this assumption is not in accord either with common experience or with what we took to be religious values. If we abandon it, the way is cleared for constructing a consistent doctrine of divine relatedness, both in its external and its internal, its absolute and its surrelative, aspects, both in its transcendent independence and in its transcendent dependence or sensitivity, its absolute or non-reflexive, and its relative or reflexive, supremacy, its A-Perfection and its R-Perfection, its non-self-surpassing, and its self-surpassing, surpassing of all others.

Bradley on External Relations

Several decades ago the subject of external relations was reopened, as a result of the contention—by F. H. Bradley and others—that relations, so far as real, are all internal. It is a violent historical paradox that this denial of external relations came from those who were styled "absolutists," and that the defense of such relations came from those who were commonly supposed to be rejecting any conception of an absolute. This confusing inversion of terminology was largely overlooked, and the result was a failure to detect the historical continuity of problems and to draw the lessons of the total historical debate.

It is true that the connection between absolute and externally related had in the Middle Ages been put indirectly rather than in so many words. Moreover, medieval thinkers had themselves identified the supreme or superlatively excellent being, God, with the pure absolute, nonrelative, independent, or nontemporal (these four terms come to the same thing). The modern absolutists correctly reasoned as follows. The supreme being must be all-inclusive, since otherwise there would be a total reality superior to the supreme, which latter would have the status of a mere constituent of this total. On the other hand, if supreme is identical with absolute or nonrelative, and yet the supreme must include all things, hence all relations, the result is a contradiction. Bradley (in his famous *Appearance and Reality*) took the heroic—or fantastic—measure of dealing with the contradiction by declaring that relations, whether internal or external, are unreal. Since there are no relations to exclude, the nonrelative need not exclude any, and thus can be all-inclusive—in the Pickwickian sense that there is nothing distinguishable for it to either exclude or include. It thus becomes not so much the total as the sole reality.

Unfortunately, few seem to have seen that the two propositions There is something absolute and There is something inclusive (or outside of which there is nothing) are not necessarily responsible for the contradiction above referred to. The contradiction may result only from the additional and really self-contradictory proposition, The nonrelative and the all-inclusive are identical. This proposition was formally rejected as "Pantheism" in the Middle Ages; but it was nevertheless implied in the medieval doctrine that absolute as such is identical with supreme. For whatever the supreme may be, it cannot be less or more than all-inclusive (the very notion that there is a better than the totality self-contradictorily posits a supertotality inclusive of the value of this "better") ; and therefore, if supreme is the same as absolute, the absolute must be all-inclusive, hence contain relations, hence be relative after all. Thus the axiom responsible for the pantheistic confusions in Spinoza and in Bradley is the very one that prevented medieval theory from solving the problem of absolute-and-relative in a consistent manner: the unfounded notion that supremely excellent means "in all respects absolute." This axiom was, to be sure, attacked by William James and others, but often without clarity on the crucial point, which is that it is one thing to identify supreme with all-inclusive, quite another to identify supreme with absolute. Absolute is identical neither with supreme nor with inclusive.

In spite of this basic confusion, on both sides of the controversy, the recent debate concerning external relations did, I think, accomplish something. By a relation to Y being external to the term X was meant that X could have been exactly the same in nature had there been no such relation to Y.[1] For example, the number two, which I think of, would have been the number two even though I had never thought of it. Also, the number two, in its formal, mathematical sense, is the number two, regardless of whether it is the number of eyes in my head or not. Had I never existed with my two eyes, two would still have been

1. See G. E. Moore's essay on "External and Internal Relations" in his *Philosophical Studies.*

one more than one, a half of four, and one less than three. To deny this independence of the mathematical two is to assert that mathematics is the study of the biographies of all persons who count to two that ever have existed or ever may exist, and (following the principle further) that there is no difference between pure mathematics, psychology, sociology, history, prophecy, physics, and so on. But on the other hand, to understand persons fully, one must know some arithmetic. The experience which has as object the number two would have been a perceptibly different experience if no such object had been given to it. To grasp the biography and individual psychology of a Bertrand Russell one would have to have a fairly deep knowledge of mathematics. But all of this knowledge, as mathematical knowledge, could be imparted to a student who was given no notion that any such person as Russell ever existed. Thus relations between numbers and persons are external to the one, but in some instances internal to the other, or at least to their experiences or states.

It may, of course, be said that the biographical part of mathematics, though a real part, is less important, for a certain purpose, than other parts. But the notion of importance is meaningless save with reference to alternatives of action and a common measure of value (the purpose spoken of) which will be identical whichever alternative is chosen—and this is again the notion of external relations. Take it how you will, external relations there must be.

Even Bradley, the philosopher who most stoutly denied the possibility of external relations, admitted and emphasized that the consequence of such denial is the reduction of all thought to self-contradiction, and of the idea of relation to an absurdity. But before yielding to this defeatist conclusion, logic is obliged to consider very carefully indeed the arguments by which it is supposed to be established.

One of Bradley's arguments against external relatedness was that it involves a vicious regress. If A is not, in its very being or identity, related to B, then we must relate A to the relation to B to get A really related. And this leads to a series of relations to relations to relations . . . a series which is vicious not only because it is infinite but because it can never arrive at a relation to B which really is A's. Is this argument sound?

I answer yes, if it is taken to prove one thing; no, if taken to prove another. It is sound if taken to prove that relations cannot be external to *all* their terms. For if no term is constituted by the relation, then the relatedness is additional to all the terms, and must be related to them by a further relation, and so on. But the argument is unsound if taken to prove relations cannot be external to any terms, that every term must be constituted by the relations in which it is. For suppose an A R B internal to A and external to B. Since the relationship is internal to A, it is nothing additional to A. A just is something-related-to-B. Thus, for example, the experience of B is not first the experience, plus relation to B, but rather there is one entity, experience-of-B. What seems to be a separable constituent in this entity, "experience," or "experience of," is not the concrete term standing in relation to B, but rather experience in general, a mere class concept or generic property. "*The* experience of" taken alone is nonsense, there is only the experience of B, or the experience of C. A different object means a different subject, if by subject we mean a concrete cognitive state. But with a different subject there may still be the same object. There can be several knowers of B, for instance, if B is the number two. True, the knowers must differ in some objects, so that really we have the knower-of-B-and-various-other-unspecified-objects.   But all this is one entity, one cognitive state. Relatedness to the

given objects is no addition to the being of the subject—
as an actual awareness or experience—but is that being.
Thus there is no regress. Only if we try to get B related to
A does the regress arise. For B, we have supposed, is not
in itself related to A. To get it so related would mean to
add, to B's mere being-B, its being-related-to-A, and this
addition would itself be a relating, and thus we would relate
B to relation to A, and so on. But the point is we do not
have to get "B related to A." An external relation is only
nominally a relation "of" the term to which it is external.
It is not that certain terms externally have relations, but
that certain relations have terms, in such fashion that the
terms, some of them, do not really "have" the relations. It
is only nominally that the term B is "in the relation," if that
means that the term has a relation of inness to the relation.
Rather, the relation possesses the term; and hence the other
term A, to which the relation is internal, in possessing the
relation, possesses the term B also. For example, XY, as a
complex, is related to X. It has X as constituent. This
"having" is the relation. But to say that X "is a constituent" had by XY is only a way of saying over again
that XY has X in a certain manner. It is the complex, not
the constituent, that here has relation. To deny this is to
deny the very ideas of analytic complex and constituent, is,
as Bradley admits, to make all rational thought and analysis self-contradictory. And, as we have seen, we need not
and should not deny it.

Internal Relations

Bradley attempts also to prove that even internal relations are inconceivable. But here, as in the other case,
though more subtly, he really substitutes for the question,
"can relations be internal to *any* terms?" the very different
question, "can they be internal to *all* terms?" Apart from

this distortion of the issue, Bradley can only be trying to get us to admit that an entity which has constituents cannot be conceived as one entity, that there can be no such thing as integration, or as something which, though itself one, yet contains a plurality. This is the point at issue, and it seems we should on no account concede it; for, as we have seen, even external relations must be internal to something; so that to give up internal relations would be to give up all relations. And would it not be absurd, on the basis of argument, which is a relating of ideas, to admit that there are no relations? We seem led to the conclusion that there are both internally and externally related terms, both terms having relation and terms which relations have without the terms in themselves having the relations.

In the end, Bradley admits there is an entity which, though one, contains many; however, he says the oneness is real and the manyness is more or less "unreal." There are many more or less unreal cases of many, and there are many degrees of unreality. Bradley is merciless enough toward traditional theology and its contradictions, yet his own position seems just as much a playing fast and loose with concepts.

The case against Bradley can be stated with reference to his famous formula: If the relation does nothing to the terms (fails to qualify or contribute to their being), it is idle; if it does modify the terms, it is vicious. To this we may reply, if the relation does nothing to a term A, it is indeed idle for that term, in the sense that it is innocuous and useless to it. But who ever thought that the purpose of studying arithmetic was to be useful to numbers? On the other hand, if the relation does something to, contributes to the being of, the term B, it need not for all that be vicious. For an enjoyment-of-arithmetic is under no necessity to be first something without relation to arithmetic and then something with this relation. Therefore, the relation does not "alter" the term, it simply is part of its being.

Absolute Terms

The conclusion that relations have both internally and externally related terms derives part of its importance from the truth that the vital absolute-relative problem is, as we have seen, connected, if not actually identical, with the problem of external and internal relations. Absolute means independent of relations, and relations of which a term is independent are those external to it, thus only nominally "its" relations. Accordingly, if every relation is internal to some, but not all, terms, then for every relation there is something absolute, so far as that relation is concerned. This gives the general and weak meaning of absolute, namely, independence of at least some relations of which the thing said to be absolute is a term. The stronger meaning, "*The* Absolute," is readily defined as the universally absolute term, the term which is absolute in *every* relation having it as term. (This, of course, is very different from Bradley's definition of the Absolute. I shall come to that.) Let us consider whether such a universally absolute term is possible.

We have taken, as the most indubitable example of an absolute term, the number two, as object of a particular human consciousness. Here is a relation which evidently does not enter into the term. This example proves two things at once: that the abstract is absolute or independent in relation to the concrete, and that the known is, or at least may be, absolute in relation to the knower. Let us consider the first-mentioned point. To say of an abstract factor of reality that it is not wholly dependent on relationships is only to say again that it is abstract. For the abstract is what can be considered while various other things are omitted from consideration. The abstract is what can be abstracted, detached in thought and, at least potentially, in actuality, from various relationships or contexts, and yet in this detachment still be the identical entity. Obviously this is the same as to say that some at least of the relations having the entity as term are external to it. This is the only intelligible meaning of absolute or independent.

That numbers are independent of our thinking them is only what we should expect from their abstractness, compared to any actual thinking. But suppose the object of awareness is concrete: for example, a past event. Does such an event contain relation to the subsequent awareness of it? Who could have discovered in the consciousness of Shakespeare any relation, however slight, to Bernard Shaw? But in the consciousness of Shaw it seems we can easily detect relation to Shakespeare. Look deeply enough into anything and you will, it may be, find its ancestors and its history inscribed upon its nature. But will you equally find its posterity and its destiny? This is the question of indeterminism, in one of its forms. There is a purely logical reason both for asserting that effects are related to causes and for denying that there is in a cause any relation whatever to ("its") *particular* future effects. Temporal relations must be somewhere, properties of something, and if particulars are not related prospectively to particulars, then they must be related retrospectively to particulars—else there would be no temporal order of particulars. But particulars cannot be related prospectively to particulars. (I agree with Ewing that relations of causal entailment do, in spite of Hume, run toward the future, but only as relations whose terms are *kinds* of particulars rather than particulars. Causal prediction concerns statistical frequencies and approximate characters, not particular events in their exact particularity.) The reason there can be no relation to future particulars is that what has relation to X has X, for X is a constituent of relation-to-X. Now if the cause has the effect, by virtue of having relation to it, then in the cause the effect *already is*, and the whole time process is the illusion of new events, whereas all events were precontained in their predecessors. This reduces the idea of time to an absurdity. On the other hand, the notion that the effect really has relation to the cause, and hence has the cause, is not similarly absurd. For change still remains, in the form of addition of new terms with their new relationships. True, the past must then still exist in the depths of the present; but this does not contradict the past's distinction from the present. For a constituent of a whole is not identical with that whole. "When the past event was present" means, on the assumption just mentioned, when the event was a whole which nothing possessed as a part; that the event is "no longer present but past" means that now a new and more inclusive whole possesses it as part. Our human consciousness has, of course, but a feeble direct awareness of the inclusion of the past in the present, via memory. But human direct awareness is not the measure of reality.

As we have seen, a whole has relation to its parts, but, unless the whole is through and through "organic"—and this cannot be if any analysis is possible—a part need not have relation to the whole. XY is not itself without X, but X may be itself without XY. "Being part" may be an external relation. Thus the present may contain the past as its relatum without thereby infecting the past with its own presentness, its own novel totality. But if the past contained this totality as its relatum, nothing novel or additional could occur.

God qua *Absolute*

An absolute term, I have held, is abstract, object, cause, predecessor, constituent, rather than concrete, subject, effect, successor, whole—in any relation in which the term is absolute. That the absolute or independent being, as such, is cause in all cause-effect relationships is traditional doctrine; also, one spoke of him as first cause, as though he were predecessor of all; but that he must also be abstract not concrete, object not subject, constituent not whole, these seem somewhat startling implications. I maintain that they follow as rigorously as the others, so far as the absolute being as such is concerned. It is worth noting too that if God (*qua* absolute) is abstract constituent of all things, then there is a clear meaning for the divine "immanence." What can more easily be in all things than something abstract? And the implication that the absolute is object for all subjects makes more sense than might appear at first thought. Here I wish to call attention to a little-noticed truth: to be known by all subjects is fully as distinctive a status as to know all objects. Take any individual other than God. It surely cannot be that this individual is known by all others. Ordinary individuals are known by their neighbors, by some few to whom they are significant; the greater the individual, the more widely will other individuals tend to take note of his existence. Only God can be so universally important that no subject can ever wholly fail or ever have failed to be aware of him (in however dim or unreflective a fashion). Thus the unique status of object-for-all-subjects is to be correlated with the more commonly recognized one of subject-for-all-objects. The difference between them is that the latter means, "having relations to all objects," and thus implies universal relativity ; the former means that all subjects have relation to the one object, without the latter having relation (other than extrinsic or nominal) to them.

Independence and Contingency

It may, indeed, appear that to be object for all subjects, as a status, must consist in a relation to all subjects, and so imply relativity. But closer attention disproves this. For the property of being such that all possible subjects will, if and when actual, have one as object involves relation, not to any particular set of subjects but to the class of possible subjects, to subjects as such. It need make no difference to the Universal Object, the Absolute, exactly which subjects are actual and therefore actually have it as object. Its universality means merely that there cannot be a subject not having it as object. But it is quite different with the universal subject. It must know which objects are actual and which merely possible; otherwise it will not "know all things," or be the universal subject. Here we have relations to actual contingent things, and such relations, being themselves contingent, render whatever contains them subject to contingency, change, dependence, relativity.

In contrast, relations to the noncontingent, to what does not first have to come into being, and can never change, constitute no threat to independence. For independence means that a thing "will be itself whether or not the thing of which it is said to be independent exists or has a certain character." But the "whether or not" refers to contingent alternatives, and is meaningless otherwise. Relationship to the necessary is in truth neither dependence nor independence, but a common property of both dependent and independent things, neutral to the distinction between them.

All things are related to the necessary. (Logicians define a necessary proposition as one "implied by every proposition," whether necessary or not.)

Independence Is Relation to the Possible as Such

Suppose one were to argue: "externally related" or "independent of relationship" is itself a relation, and thus a thing can be independent of relation-to-X only if X is there as term of this independence relation. Thus the independent is dependent, and there is a contradiction. I venture to think this a sophistry. For the absoluteness of the term in question is not, strictly speaking, with respect to relation to X, but with respect to a *kind* of relation, which can be defined, as logicians say, intensionally, or without mentioning X. Thus arithmetic is independent, not merely of my awareness of it, but of any particular awareness. Nothing is added to this attribution of independence by saying, "and also arithmetic is independent of my awareness." This is not an addition, but a mere illustration. Accordingly, it seems clear that absoluteness does not require relation to particular or actual terms. As for relation to an intensional class of terms, this constitutes no dependence, no departure from absoluteness; for the ultimate intensional classes are noncontingent, whereas the relativity negated by absoluteness is relativity to the contingent. The ultimate possibilities are as such necessarily real (even though not "actual"). They could not possibly have failed to be the possibilities which they are, and it is with reference to them that absoluteness is defined, not with reference to actuality. Independence of relationship is neutrality or indifference to relational alternatives, so that any possible relation must, if actualized, be compatible with the term in its entire nature. Hence it "makes no difference" to the term which relations are actualized.

If the foregoing is correct, then to achieve a consistent idea of "absolute" we need not attempt the impossible task of abstracting from all relationships, but only of abstracting from relationships to particular contingent things. This is by no means impossible. The number "two" involves no particular things whatsoever. If it be objected that there could be no such thing as two were there no contingent particulars, no actual couples, the reply is that this, if granted, would only mean that to conceive two is to conceive that the class of particular contingent things is not empty and has at least two members; and it is one thing to say that every existent member of the class of particular things exists contingently and another to say it is contingent that there are some members of the class or other. It may be necessary, not contingent, that there be some contingent things or other. The existence of the human race may be contingent in the sense that the totality of existence might not have contained the human race; but it does not follow that the totality of contingent existence might have been zero. The contingency of each member of the class of contingent existence means that there might have been no member just like it; but the class itself may have been necessarily represented by some members or other. If not this, then that; if not that, then the other. Still otherwise expressed, there are various alternative possibilities, but perhaps all possibilities are positive. There is then no such thing as the possibility that no possibility be actualized. There is no possibility of "nothing contingent," but only of this contingent thing or that contingent thing or some other contingent thing (other than sheer nothing). I believe this is the correct view, though I shall not attempt to prove its correctness in this book.

The import of the foregoing is that the absoluteness of God need not imply his nonrelationship to the creation *as such,* but only to the contingent alternatives of creation. Every creature may be contingent, in that some other creature was possible instead of it, but "no creation whatever" may not be a possibility. In that case, God might be essentially "creator," incapable of not creating, though perfectly capable of not creating this or that creature— any creature you choose. Admitting free alternatives of creation does not force one to admit "not creating anything" as one of the alternatives. Hence there is no absurdity in the idea that God is relative to creation as such, that he is *bound* to create, provided he is not thus bound with respect to any given creature or set of them. In this way we escape the otherwise embarrassing questions: Why is there a world? Could the absolute have refrained from producing the relative? Since absolute is defined in terms of relativity, as such, it cannot be independent of relativity in every sense, but it can be independent of *which* relative things there are.

The Independence of Enduring Individuals

We have considered external relations between abstract and concrete, and between past and present. Suppose now we consider the relations of individuals with self-identity through time, say, individual animals to their environments. To say of such an enduring individual that it is independent of its environment can only mean this: with respect to certain abstract qualities, the individual is the same regardless of changes around it. All concrete enduring things have *some* independence in this sense. Thus a man will be a "human being," regardless, within wide limits, of what happens. He will not lose his essential humanity and basic personality traits because of ordinary changes in weather, scenery, or other surroundings. But every change in weather or scenery alters, more or less drastically, the concrete flow of sensations entering into the person's experience. And extreme changes in weather or scenery might temporarily or permanently rob even Abraham Lincoln of his moral humaneness. The partial independence of a good man's goodness (the abstract quality, "being good" as such) with respect to varying relationships may, then, be taken as the "weak" analogue of the absolute independence of the divine goodness as such with respect to all contingencies. Thus God will be good no more and no less if this happens than if that happens instead. But it clearly does not follow that his more concrete qualities will be unchanged. It is one concrete act to be good to Robinson, if Robinson sins greatly, another to be good to him if he is as righteous as man may be. Yet the goodness of the divine treatment of Robinson may be the same in degree or eminence.

Another abstract quality that permits independence is wisdom. A shrewd man may be about equally shrewd in facing heat and cold, sickness and health, friend and foe. Similarly, but eminently, God may be all-knowing and all-wise regardless of what facts there are to know. Be the facts these and these, he knows these and these; be they those and those, he knows those and those; either way his omniscience is fully preserved. But the concrete knowledge which he has is by no means the same; for it is sheer contradiction to say that the knowledge that P is true is the *same* as the knowledge that P is not true. He who infallibly knows P is true cannot be concretely and in all respects the same subject as he who infallibly knows P is false; indeed the existence of either subject excludes the existence of the other. Thus an actual divine knowing cannot be exclusive of relations, cannot be wholly absolute.

Supreme as All-inclusive

To include relations is to include their terms. Hence to know all is to include all. Thus we must agree with modern absolutism and orthodox Hinduism that the supreme being must be all-inclusive. The only way to keep both the absoluteness and the inclusive knowledge required by the religious idea is to restrict the absoluteness to an abstract aspect or dimension of the supreme being. The supreme in its total concrete reality will be the supereminent case of relativity, the Surrelative, just as, in its abstract character it will be the supereminent case of nonrelativity—not only absolute, but *the* absolute. Now it is in truth just as easy to define a strong or eminent, as contrasted to a weak or ordinary, sense of the term relative as of the term absolute. The superior listener to the poem, in our illustration in the previous chapter, is indeed relative, in his flow of thought and feeling, to the reading of the poem. But many other poems, perhaps, are being read in the world, and toward these other readings the given listener is impassive, unrelated, absolute, independent. They affect him not, for he does not hear them; and many of them could not greatly affect him, for they are in unknown languages. Thus to be relative in the weak sense is to be related to a mere portion of the actual totality of terms permitting such relativity, and not to all aspects even of these (for not all the possible contributions even of one poem are received by any one hearer). To be relative in the eminent sense will (accordingly) be to enjoy relations to all that is, in all its aspects. Supreme dependence will thus reflect all influences—with infinite sensitivity registering relationship to the last and least item of events. Is this not genuinely something eminent and supreme? Could any man exhibit such sensitivity, or anything remotely approaching it? Obviously not. Indeed, only an all-knowing being can, in any intelligible sense, be thus supremely relative to all beings. For such relativity means that every difference makes a difference *in* the all-relative one, that for every diversity anywhere there is a diversity of relationships *in* him. Only the conception of an intuition whose datum is the universe gives any positive meaning to such an idea. Mere "matter," supposed to be the most passive of entities, must really be the most *im*passive, if passivity means ability to reflect difference in other things. The closer we get to a "merely material" individual, the closer we come to something for which nearly all changes in the universe make no appreciable difference at all. The impassivity of a turtle is great compared to that of a man, but that of a bit of moss is greater still, and it is exceeded by that of a bit of rock. Only the crudest or nearest alterations of other things produce change in relationships perceptible as changes *in* the bit of rock itself. But a man can be put into agonies or ecstasies by some subtle shift in human thought on the other side of the world, or even a thousand years in the past.

The Principle of Eminence

The foregoing procedure of identifying a weak sense of absoluteness and also relativity, and attributing these, in eminent sense, to deity illustrates what has been called in theology the "way of eminence." Whatever is good in the creation is, in superior or eminent fashion, "analogically not univocally," the property of God. Thus knowledge, purpose, life, love, joy, are deficiently present in us, eminently and analogically present in God. It is only in this manner that the idea of God acquires any positive meaning controllable by analysis, and yet free from anthropomorphic crudities. Opposed to the positive way of eminence and analogy is the famous negative theology, the *via negativa,* which proceeds by "removing" predicates as unworthy of application to God. This negative way was never consistently followed out, yet, in so far as followed, it interfered with the consistent use of the way of eminence. Whereas the way of eminence, if consistently executed, treats the categories *impartially*, the way of negation plays favorites among the categories. Thus there is a weak or ordinary sense of independence of relationships and a supreme or eminent sense which was applied to God. But although there is similarly a weak or ordinary sense of relativity, the eminent form was not attributed to God. Impossible, said theologians, for relativity is bad in principle; only independence is good in essence. Similarly, cause is good and God is eminently cause; but effect is bad or essentially inferior, and there is no eminent effect. This procedure is scandalously illogical and arbitrary. First, it is just as easy, as we shall see, to conceive an eminent sense of effect as of cause. Second, cause itself, at least in the form of conscious or voluntary cause, implies relation to effect so far as these are known and valued by the cause. Third, if or in so far as the cause does not contain relation to the effect and thus is not relative with respect to it, then it is the effect (or something not the cause) which contains relation to the cause. But it follows that in comparing cause and effect we are not comparing two entities, C and E, each outside of the other, but rather a C and an E^C, a cause alone and an effect-with-a-cause, a part and a whole. And traditional doctrine declared unwittingly that the part is greater than the whole! Fourth, if effect as such is inferior to cause as such, then since later is to earlier as effect to cause, process as such is transition to the inferior, and is essentially degeneration!

An Eminent Effect

I said above that it is quite possible to conceive an eminent case of *effect*. Effects are better or worse; and Plato long ago showed how to formulate the idea of an eminent effect or creation. The animate creature is superior to the inanimate, the rational animal to the nonrational. Moreover, the universe as an effect is superior to all other effects, as the whole or inclusive effect is superior to parts or included effects. Suppose then that the universe is, in eminent fashion, animate and rational. It will, accordingly, be supreme among effects. All other creatures will be its members, inferior as such. For instance, all else will depend, as it will not, upon an *external* environment. Thus the universe, patterned after the ideal of rational animality, will be as distinctive among effects as the creator of the universe is distinctive among causes. If the universe is *not* patterned thus, the creator did not do a good job of creating. He created something inferior (in principle and not just in degree) to what he might have created. On the other hand, if the universe is eminently animate and rational, then either it is God, or there are two eminent beings, God and Universe, and a third supereminent entity, which is the total reality of God-and-universe. The dilemma is satisfactorily dissolved only by the admission that the God who creates and the inclusive creation are one God. Then the two eminences under cause and effect are two aspects of God rather than two Gods, or than a God and an eminent being other than God.

Abstract and Concrete in God

If Cornford and Demos are right, the two Gods in the *Timaeus*, the creator God and created God, or the "eternal God and the God that was to be," are aspects of one and the same deity. God in one aspect is creator, in another and more complete aspect is both creator and created, is both concrete world-soul and abstract eternal reason by which the world-soul inspires itself and all lesser beings. The merely eternal God is the element of sheer rational purpose. This element is indeed absolute, unaffected by contingent relationships. But the concrete acts which achieve the eternal purpose can do so only by embracing within themselves all contingent relationships. These concrete acts are analogous to those of a human person; as the abstract eternal purpose is analogous to the underlying general purpose a man may pursue throughout his life, or to the enduring "character" a man exhibits under diverse circumstances and through diverse experiences, sensations, feelings. The basic difference between man and God can be seen in this, that whereas the character individual to a man cannot be stated in merely abstract terms, such as good or wise or perverse or foolish (all such abstractions being, for all that could be known, applicable to other individuals), God's character, on the contrary, can be described in utterly abstract terms which yet are unique to him as the one divine individual. Only one individual can ever be omniscient, primordial-and-everlasting, all-loving, supreme cause of all effects, supreme effect of all causes. Only one individual can ever be divine. Here is an extremely abstract character which yet is the defining characteristic of a self —or person. This character, though individual to God, is so abstract or nonspecific that it can be correlated with any possible character you please in its correlate, the world. Whatever the world may be, God can know that world in his uniquely adequate way, whereas some possible worlds would exclude human knowers altogether. The utter abstractness of the individual essence of God is what makes him, as concrete individual, completely independent of relational alternatives for his mere existence. Because the defining character of his self-identity is utterly neutral to such alternatives, the concrete embodiment can be wholly expressive of and variable with relations. The character can be expressed in any relational pattern, hence God can contain any relational pattern and still be himself.

To combine in one's individuality the extremes of abstract and concrete, universal independence or nonrelativity and universal dependence or sensitivity, is to have maximal security and value as an individual. To be sure, the character of sensitivity, or *non*neutrality to alternatives, is always, even in ordinary cases, as an abstraction, something more or less independent or neutral. Partiality does not itself play favorites; only partial subjects do that. Not kindness but kind persons respond variously to varying needs. However, incomplete kindness is never wholly independent, since any personal form of such incompleteness (for example, mine or yours) will impose local conditions without which it cannot be concretized. Only contingent conditions can individualize inadequate relational forms. Complete or adequate sensitivity, on the contrary, is *ipso facto* individual or personal, hence in its individuality neutral to conditions. It will be adequate to any possible such conditions, hence can exist in any with its own defining individuality. To be wholly match for this environment is to be potentially match for any possible environment. It remains none the less true that matching one environment is not the same concrete act as matching another. The "environment" here is an internal one, meaning field of operations or relational acts whose terms are fully possessed. Such full possession makes them in the strictest sense internal, but does not prevent their being terms and the relations being relations. They are supreme relations. That which is thus supremely related is far from "unmoved" or independent of becoming; it is rather, at all times, unfailingly and adequately moved. Hence its adequacy, its unfailing sensitivity, is unmoved, and is indeed the unmoved mover of all movable things—including God himself as concrete individual.

The difference between ordinary and divine relativity can be expressed in many ways. One way is this: God is relative, but what we may call the extent of his relativity is wholly independent of circumstances, wholly nonrelative. Regardless of circumstances, of what happens anywhere or when, God will enjoy unrestricted cognitive relativity to all that coexists with him. By contrast, the extent of our human relativity is itself a relative matter, varying with circumstances. It varies all the way from the minimal cognitive relatedness of a man in deep sleep, or the zero cognitive relatedness of a dead man, to the maximal reflection of objects in full waking consciousness of a man in perfect condition and mental development. Now there is a difference of logical level between simple relativity, and relativity as to extent and endurance of relativity. God is completely without the latter or second-order relativity in his own character (save in the sense in which the characters of included relata are contained in the character of the including relative term). Thus exact analysis shows that we are not obliterating the uniqueness of deity by affirming his relativity. We can even call ours a "negative theology," in that second-order relativity, "relativity of relativity," is in this theology denied of deity, though affirmed of all other beings. God is not, it is true, *simpliciter* "independent"; but the generic manner or universal extent of his dependence is his unique and wholly independent possession. With us, the extent of our dependence is also radically dependent, and our very existence as dependent is wholly a matter of chance or contingency.

The Absolute as Less than God

Let us sum up the position we have reached. Medieval and modern realists are right, we have contended, in positing a one-sided relativity of subject to object; but the medieval reversal of this relativity in the case of the divine knower is unnecessary and untenable. What is necessary is that, as subject knowing all things, and as immutable absolute, God should not, in every sense, be identically the same entity. Rather, in conceiving God as absolute, we must recognize that we are abstracting from his actual subjectivity or knowing. The Absolute is God with something left out of account. God is more than his absolute character. There is no contradiction; for we have defined absolute to mean non-relative, and this meaning does not coincide with that of "all-inclusive" or "supreme." Nor can it mean anything more than the supreme, for that would be nonsense. Accordingly, it can only mean something less than the supreme, as such. In this we are affirming the contrary of the Hindu doctrine (rejected by Ramanuja and others), which is sometimes asserted also in the West, that the personal God of worship is a more or less unreal appearance of the absolute. I am arguing that the absolute is, rather, an abstract feature of the inclusive and supreme reality which is precisely the personal God. If one must speak of "appearance," then the absolute, simply as such, may be termed the appearance of ultimate reality to abstract cognition, including the divine self-cognition in its abstract aspect. The absolute is not more, but less, than God—in the obvious sense in which the abstract is less than the concrete.

Some Absolutistic Arguments

In defense of the view that the absolute or independent can be concrete and all-inclusive, it is sometimes said that what includes everything cannot depend upon anything, for there is nothing outside itself to depend upon. However, independence of this "nothing" outside the all-inclusive is as little total independence as there is absence of rancor in the fact that one does not hate the man in the moon—there being no man in the moon. A whole is not identical with its constituents, and to depend upon constituents is a very real dependence indeed, as we human beings, with our many-factored bodies, ought to realize, and as medieval thought had the merit of never forgetting. Thus it is truly Pickwickian to guarantee independence on the ground that any dependence must be internal. Change the least item in a totality, and it is not the same totality. If all changeable things are such items, then the totality is of all things the most changeable.

The counterargument that the totality of changes cannot change is not acceptable. For the totality of changes can very well change, by the addition of new changes, previously unactualized. The objection that the totality of changes must include all future changes too is to be met by the question, what could be meant by future change if there is now or eternally a complete totality, never to be increased, of changes? Then nothing new really occurs, everything is as old as eternity and as immutable. The only way to free the idea of time from paradox is to admit, with Bergson, that time is creation, creation of events which exist neither eternally nor at all times but only from and after the time of their creation or occurrence. This means that the totality of events as including a given event is a new totality produced by or coming into being with that event.

Another unacceptable argument is that the dependence which absoluteness denies is with respect to something contingent, and in reality nothing is contingent, everything is necessary. But in that case, we should never be able to assert either necessity or contingency, since neither term can have any meaning save in correlation and contrast with the other. Here we may observe that if all individuals are necessary, then all aggregates are also, that if the concrete is necessary, then so is anything abstract which it contains, so that the only way to permit any application for the indispensable contrasting term, contingent, is to give up the assertion that all individuals are necessary. It is notably otherwise with the assertion that all individuals, say, are subjects. For it would not follow that all aggregates of individuals are subjects; since an aggregate of individuals need not be an individual, in the sense of a well-unified singular, and an aggregate of subjects certainly need not be a subject. Still more obvious is it that an abstract aspect of a subject need not be a subject. The very character of subjectivity as such, as an abstraction, is no subject. Thus the argument, often used against any form of idealism, that he who says all individuals are subjects is depriving the term subject of contrast, hence of meaning, is not a valid argument. But in the case of necessity, it really would destroy all contrast and meaning to assert that every individual or concrete singular is necessary, or, as "absolutists" sometimes do, to assert that there are no individuals save the one necessary one.

Another device for justifying the use of language involved in calling "absolute"—which historically meant independent or nonrelative—that which is all-inclusive consists in declaring that relations are unreal or inconceivable, and since there are no relations, the all-inclusive need neither contain nor exclude them. This seems to amount to saying that the relation of appearance and reality—for relations at least *appear*—is the only relation, and is somehow not really a relation. Further, as Bradley and others admit, if relations are given up, everything thinkable is given up, and we are left with the mystic silence. And it would still be true that the all-inclusive at least appears to be the most relative of all things, for it appears to be related to all the appearances of relation, whereas other things appear to be related to but some of them.

Still another argument for "absolutism" might be that the absolutely all-inclusive and absolutely independent agree in being—absolute. But note that "absolutely" is an adverb, not an adjective. Note also that absolutely independent is better expressed as wholly independent, independent in all relationships. Note finally that one may also speak of the absolutely dependent, dependent in all relationships. Is it not dangerous to shift from diverse uses of the term absolute in this fashion? Should we not adhere to independent or nonrelational as the meaning of the adjective absolute, and employ another word, like all-inclusive, when that is what we mean? And what is to prove that the supreme instance of independence will coincide with the supreme instance of inclusiveness? We have seen that the exact opposite is what we should expect, namely, that the all-inclusive will be the least absolute thing there is.

The Relative as Including the Absolute

But, though the all-inclusive cannot, in its inclusiveness, *be* absolute, yet, since it includes all things, it can perfectly well *include* something absolute. For to be included is, we have argued, an external relation, a relation of which the included is a term, but not a subject. Therefore, the absolute can exist in the supremely relative, in serene independence, serene exemption from relativity. For it is not the absolute which has the relation, "in" the actual relative, but rather and only the relative which has the relation, "containing" the absolute; just as it is the particular subject which has the cognitive relation to the object, while the latter is only nominally "in" this relation. And, indeed, since an abstraction cannot actually know, it can only, when we speak of it, be something known, an object. Thus the absolute is a divine object in the divine subject and for the divine subject. It is an essence, not an existence. Nevertheless, it may yet be that God's existence follows from his essence, if by "his existence" we mean only that there is some existence embodying the divine essence. For while the object is independent of any particular subject, it is not independent of subjectivity as such; just as the abstract is neutral with regard to alternatives of concrete embodiment but is not neutral to the alternative, some embodiment or none. That God exists is one with his essence and is an analytic truth (as I hope to show elsewhere), but how, or in what actual state of experience or knowledge or will, he exists is contingent in the same sense as is our own existence. Thus at long last we do justice to the distinction between essence and existence without rendering the truth that there is a divine existence contingent, a mere fact, subject to accident or possible nullification. At long last we can be existentialists in theology, without denying the serene independence of that in God which is bound to be embodied in existence. At long last we can accept theologically the logical axiom that actuality is of a different logical type from any predicate, but yet maintain that "existence," as meaning merely that there is some actual embodiment of the predicate, may be necessary.

In terms of the principles we have set forth, the absolute character of God must be something which is not determinate subject for any object, which is not particular under a universal, or species under a genus, and is not datable as subsequent to anything. It might seem that it must coincide with pure being, of which these statements are also true. And indeed, God in his absolute character is Being itself, in the sense which abstracts from all particular determinations. The character of omniscience (and other divine attributes, which are mutually equivalent) is no "particular" determination, since it is describable through categories alone. Neither is the character of "world" as such determinate; for it merely means whatever is not omniscient. Since the omniscient as such knows whatever else exists, the non-omniscient is contained in the omniscient as known in the knower. Thus the form of pure being is the divine subjectivity as such (not any actual divine subject) as including the divine objectivity or content as such. This common reference to the divine is a univocal aspect of pure being. But there is also an "analogical" aspect; for the all-knowingness of God is categorically diverse from the ignorance of his objects, and the including is diverse from the included.

In terms of the same principles, the surrelative actuality of God is the highest actualized level of concreteness, subject surveying all actual objects, event subsequent to all actual events not contemporaneous with it. In this aspect, God is not pure being but total actual being of a given moment, with all achieved determinations. Thus God is being in both its opposite aspects: abstract least common denominator, and concrete de facto maximal achieved totality.

Surrelativism and Panentheism

Is surrelativism a pantheistic doctrine? Not if this means a doctrine which denies the personality of deity; nor yet if it means that deity is identical with a mere collection of entities, as such, even the cosmic collection. The total actual state of deity-now, as surrelative to the present universe, has nothing outside itself, and in that sense is the All. But the individual essence of deity (what makes God God, or the divine divine) is utterly independent of this All, since any other possible all (and there are infinite possibilities of different totalities) would have been compatible with this essence. The divine personal essence in this fashion infinitely transcends the de facto totality, and every moment a partly new totality contains and embodies the essence. (We have throughout contended that the "contained" need not depend on what contains it.) The error of most pantheists has been to deny the externality of concrete existence to the essence of deity. They have not realized that the inclusive actuality of God, which includes all de facto actuality, is as truly contingent and capable of additions as the least actuality it includes. This is the freedom both of God and of the creatures. For since the essence of God is compatible with any possible universe, we can be allowed some power of decision, as between possibilities, without infringing the absolute independence of God in his essential character or personality. And God's own freedom is likewise safeguarded, since freedom means a personal character with which alternative concrete experiences or states are compatible. True, the actual state of deity will be determined partly by the creatures; but this is simply the social character of the divine self-decision, and it is hard to know what to do with opponents who almost in one breath accuse one of an "impersonal" idea of deity and yet object to the admission of social relativity, a basic aspect of personality, in the divine person.

If "pantheism" is a historically and etymologically appropriate term for the view that deity is the all of relative or interdependent items, with nothing wholly independent or in any clear sense nonrelative, then "panentheism" is an appropriate term for the view that deity is in some real aspect distinguishable from and independent of any and all relative items, and yet, taken as an actual whole, includes all relative items. Traditional theism or deism makes God

solely independent or noninclusive. Thus there are logically
the three views: (1) God is merely the cosmos, in all aspects
inseparable from the sum or system of dependent things
or effects; (2) he is both this system and something independent of it; (3) he is not the system, but is in all aspects
independent. The second view is panentheism. The first
view includes any doctrine which, like Spinoza's, asserts
that there is a premise from which all facts are implied conclusions. A proposition means whatever follows from it, and
it is contradictory or meaningless to say that God is independent of all things because he necessitates them. Effects
imply their causes (whether or not causes do their effects)
and what implies particulars is logically on the level of the
effect or the dependent, not of the independent. Panentheism agrees with traditional theism on the important point
that the divine individuality, that without which God would
not be God, must be logically independent, that is, must not
involve any particular world. The distinction between individual and state, or personality and experience, enables
us to combine this point of theism with the equally necessary point of traditional pantheism that God cannot in his
full actuality be less or other than literally all-inclusive.
This view is exactly as far from traditional pantheism as
from traditional theism, and therefore I suggest it would be
ignorance or bad faith to call it pantheism. A suitable term
has been proposed (not first by me). I scarcely need to say
that surrelativism and panentheism are logically the same
doctrine with only a difference of emphasis.

One important reason for not giving up the notion that
God literally contains the universe is derived from the theory of value. If A contains the value of B and also some
additional value, then the value of A exceeds that of B. This
is perhaps the only assumption that makes "better" self-
evident.

We overlook this sometimes for the reason that, instead of asking, Does this experience (say of a man) literally include that (say, of an insect) and more besides? we ask rather, Does the human experience include the abstract species of value imaginable for the insect, while the converse is not true? Thus insect and man have senses, but only man has linguistic symbols and all that they add to experience. Now it is on this route—with some deviations—that people have tried often to conceive the superiority of deity. Not that God literally has our enjoyments, oh no, not even that he has their abstract equivalents. But he has something better. He has not our form of enjoyment, but he has enjoyment—or "bliss"—on a radically higher level. Just so, thought is superior to sensation. But thought as we know it includes sensation. If it did not, how could thought, or anything, know the superiority of thought? Moreover, we must recognize that if a man is superior to an insect, a world containing insect and man is superior somehow to either alone. Each somehow adds, we feel, to the richness of existence. The reason is that it is only abstractly that human sense is equivalent to the insect's. Concretely there must be some value in insect sensations that we miss. We have something else, as good or better, but nevertheless a world containing both is better still. I fail to see any well-authenticated principle of value that justifies us in assuming a divine instance which, without literal containing of all experiences, has the equivalent of all their values.

Similar remarks ought to be made about the familiar contention that if God is a person he must have other persons "over against" or "outside" of him. If he "has" them, he has them, and that is the clear meaning of containing. That we "have things outside us" is because we have without having, because we only abstractly enjoy their values, or only with inefficient, faint awareness beyond the reach of introspection. Is that the way to conceive God, as similarly failing effectively to have his relations and their relata? God as personal must have relations and relata, and he must actually and effectively have these.

The same criterion proves that in some sense God must be in man. If it is possible to have a distinct idea of man without any awareness of God, then how could God possibly be inferred? And if it is not possible, then surely the being of man includes that of God. It does not effectively include it, and hence we do not rival God in value. What we can clearly infer as to God is only his abstract essence, and the wholly abstract is no actual value. The concrete actuality of God is in us only in so far as we, with radical ineffectiveness or faintness, intuit it. Though it is vastly less true to say that we do than that we do not "have" or include God, both statements are true. God, on the other hand, in his actual or relative aspect, unqualifiedly or with full effectiveness has or contains us; while in his absolute aspect he is the least inclusive of all individuals.

Higher Synthesis of Absolutism and Pluralism

Our doctrine must partially contradict, not only scholasticism and nineteenth-century absolute idealism, but also a large majority of the realistic critics of absolutism. These men—for example, William James—apparently thought that if there are external relations, there is no all-inclusive reality. This appears not to follow. For to say that there is something all-inclusive is to say there is something that contains and is thus related to all other things; but from this it cannot be deduced that all other things are related either to the inclusive thing or to each other. True, all are contained, and co-contained, in the inclusive being, but the question is whether this relation of "being contained" or of "being co-

contained" is a nominal, external, or a real, internal, relation. It must be an external relation; for if the included
things have relation to the including thing, then, since "to
have the relation is to have the term," they would include
the including thing, and all distinction between including
and included would vanish. Thus, only if some relations are
external, can there, in a significant sense, be an all-inclusive
reality!

As the reader is perhaps recalling, it was said above that
man contains God, and that God contains man. How then
is there distinction between including and included? The
reply must be somewhat complex. First, as was explained
above, cognitive relativity has intensive as well as extensive
degrees; thus man, though extensively he is as inclusive as
God (so far as coexistent with man), intensively is not so.
But second, this intensive difference would be meaningless
without some extensive difference of inclusiveness. For to
say that God does while we do not effectively embrace the
universe coexistent with us is to say that the universe, without any one of us, might have been little different in value,
whereas its value would have been radically different given
an equally radical difference in the concrete actuality of
God. But this comparison implies that there is a meaning to
"universe without us"; also that the concrete actuality of
God could have been otherwise; finally, that "value" has a
meaning not dependent upon our existence; and nothing
of all this could be admitted were there no external relations. Where all items are strictly necessary to each other's
being, there can be no question how important a given item
is in comparison to another. Degrees of importance imply
dispensability, nonnecessity, external relationship somewhere. Third, even extensively God is more inclusive than
man in that the God who coexists with man is only God dur-

ing a certain portion of his everlasting endurance. Prior to the beginning of this portion, God included all that then was or had been, while man included nothing—for there was no man. Subsequent to the end of the portion, God will include all that now is plus all that then may be, much of which man will never include at all, however faintly or ineffectively. So God, in his relative aspect, is the only unqualifiedly inclusive being, as, in his absolute aspect, he is the only unqualifiedly exclusive one.

Some at least of the critics of absolutism seem to have thought that if there are external relations there is nothing absolute, in the sense of independent and immutable. Since independent means externally related, this is an odd conclusion to draw. It could only have been drawn because the absolutists had confused together independent—or immutable—with all-inclusive; and their critics apparently took their word for the validity of this identification. The existence of external relations does not conflict either with there being something absolute or with there being something inclusive; but it does conflict with the notion that the all-inclusive (which must include relations, if such exist) can *be* the absolute. Through this identification absolute idealism lost the chance to convey its insight into the inclusiveness of the supreme; just as, through the identification of supremely good and absolute, scholasticism lost the chance to convey its insight into the importance, for theology, of external or nominal relatedness. We must combine the following assertions: the idea of the supreme being connotes absoluteness; it connotes, therefore, external relations; it also connotes relativity, internal relations, and all-inclusiveness. That this involves no contradiction the present chapter has sought to show. The third chapter will apply these results to the problems of the divine knowledge, goodness, and power.

Appendix to Chapter II
Relativity and Logical Entailment

To define, with anything like ideal clarity, the notions of internal and external relations would require more elaborate logical technique than this book attempts to employ. Some suggestions may, however, be offered. (This appendix adds no major step to the argument but seeks only to indicate how certain steps can be rendered more precise. It may readily be omitted by readers not primarily interested in logical technicalities.)

In the foregoing discussions, we have employed G. E. Moore's definition of external relations as those such that the entity said to be externally related could have been the same had the relations not obtained. In Chapter I, another definition was suggested: external is the negative of internal, and internal relations are ontological correlates of logical relations of "strict implication" or entailment. This seems to agree with Moore's definition. For that which the conception of a thing entails is that without which the entity could not be itself, the entity conceived. It follows that the more the conception of a thing involves that of other things, the more it is relative to those other things. To be independent, non-relative, absolute, is to be meager in logical content; the maximum of relativity is the maximum of logical content. From this we can reach the same conclusions as before concerning what sorts of entities are relative and what sorts are not. Plainly the universal or abstract is meager in logical content. The most universal conceptions, such as that of "something," affirm the least of any. "This is something" surely is a minimal affirmation, if it can be called such at all. Similarly, to say that a thing is some sort of object for some sort of subject is to say as little as possible about the thing. It may be abstract or concrete, unitary or a mere collection or class. Indeed, it may be anything you please. So "object-in-general" is equivalent to "being-in-general" in meagerness of content. It is not quite the same with "subject-in-general." For, while what is thought of or known may be either universal or particular, only a particular subject can think or know. The abstract or universal we can really think of, but it does not really think. "This is a subject" is thus richer in logical content than, "this is an object." Moreover, even "this is object for such and such a subject" still leaves the nature of the object extremely indeterminate. The same subject may have as objects things radically diverse, including universals as well as particulars, individuals as well as collections or aggregates. In contrast, "such and such an entity is object for this subject" tells us something determinate about this subject, that it knows (to some extent at least) a certain suchness, that of the object. The subject is colored by its particular objects; the object is not colored by its particular subjects. Above all, we must note that the more exact and complete the knowledge, the richer the implications for the subject of ascribing to it a certain object, and the more meager the implications for the object of ascribing to it the status of being known. Exact and complete knowledge must enjoy all the characters of the known as characters which it knows; but to say that X is known to the exact and complete knowledge tells nothing whatever about the distinctive character of X as compared to anything else in the universe. For anything else must also be known by the complete knowledge, if there be such. So we reach once more our position that the relative is the concrete, particular, and subjective; the nonrelative is the abstract, universal, and objective.

That the earlier is more meager in content than the later is less obvious, but reasons can be given for holding that it is the generic character of process to enrich the sum of determinateness. This Bergsonian-Whiteheadian view at least has two merits; that of furnishing an interpretation, otherwise lacking, for the intuitive sense that time has a directional flow or irreversibility, and that of giving an intelligible answer to the question, why process, why cannot things just exist, and be done with it? As to the first point, if it is the generic meaning of process that determinations be enriched, then a process back to an earlier or less rich state would be a contradiction in terms. As to the second point, if process enriches the determinateness of existence, then since esthetic value varies with such determinateness, process can add to the total value of existence. And if it be still asked, Why does not all possible determinateness exist once for all? the answer of course is, Because there are mutually incompatible determinations, so that the notion of an absolute maximum is here meaningless. These are by no means all the advantages or evidences that can be adduced for the doctrine that "later" means "richer determination, inclusive of the determination called earlier." And since the externally related is the meager in content, the earlier is without internal relatedness to the later, save in certain abstract causal features which, being common to earlier and later, do not constitute increased richness in the later.

According to Whitehead's philosophy, every successor prehends its predecessor, and it prehends abstract factors of being, which are common to it and some earlier events; also, there is a sense in which each earlier particular is a universal, or matrix of universals, with respect to later particulars. "Thinking about Washington" is a universal, of which "X thinks about Washington" is an instance. The existence of Washington, as an individual, is the necessary condition of there being any possibility of thinking about Washington. So each new individual implies new universals which later events may instance. Since, then, the universal is never genuinely relative to any given particular, earlier events are not relative to later events, for were they so, the universals based on them must also be thus relative. If Washington were relative to Truman (who thinks about Washington), then thinking about Washington would also be relative to Truman, and this cannot be, since Truman is a particular value of "X thinks about Washington." (It would seem to follow that if Washington thinks about Washington, then the two Washingtons are not wholly identical, also, that it is not possible for X and Y each to think about the other. To this latter problem we shall return presently.)

If Whitehead's doctrine is right, there is only one general case of external relatedness, with three inseparable aspects: the particular, succeeding subject prehends the more general, preceding object; and this relation relativizes the particular prehender to the prehended, the successor to the predecessor, the particular to the general, but *not* conversely.

This brings us to the very difficult problem, for me *the* problem, of relations between contemporaries. If the subject is always more particular than the object, then two subjects cannot be objects to each other, unless something could be meant by saying that each was, in some respect, more particular than the other. Two men could readily know each other, for a man is not one particular but a stream or system of actual and potential particular experiences. But two experiences, two momentary or irreducible "subjects," could not, according to our principles—unless some subtle qualification of them is possible—each know the other. According to physics, contemporary events are mutually independent. The only likely alternative seems to be that they are mutually interdependent. With the past there is no *inter*action, and none with the future (taking, as I believe we should, the position that causes are not dependent upon their precise and particular effects, but effects are dependent upon, relative to, their precise causes); and contemporaries, it seems, must either have no action of either one upon the other, or there must be action both ways. How could this be? Suppose a subject S knows a contemporary C. This, according to our principles, would not, of itself, mean any relativity of C to S. But perhaps there is also a reverse relation of C to S other than the non-genuine one of merely being known by S. Suppose C is another subject, S^2, and S^2 knows that itself is known by S^1. There would then be mutual awareness between C and S. Each would enter into the other, not merely as knower but as known-knower. Everything known, even a knower of oneself as known, is constitutive of the knower by which it is known. The topic of contemporary relations bristles with difficulties, and I shall only say that *if* I could find a consistent analysis of it, I should be able to die content, so far as philosophical achievements are concerned. At present the topic seems the most vulnerable point in the surrelativist doctrine. However, the difficulty would not, I think, be disposed of by dropping theism, or by returning to orthodoxy; for it is the problem of conceiving one aspect of the structure of time.

That the nonrelative is whatever is such that its conception does not entail the conception of other things agrees with the old formula for "substance": that the conception of which does not involve the conception of anything else; or that which exists and is conceived through itself alone. But when Spinoza tries to identify this logically independent factor with the concrete totality, necessitating all things as a triangle necessitates angles equal to 180 degrees, he reduces his doctrine to logical rubbish. He is saying that one essence or nature entails no other nature and yet entails every other nature. If it be objected that it is the concrete which contains within itself all that it requires to exist, the reply is that it does indeed do so; but only because it contains within itself relationships to a whole system of other concrete things. Once more, "within" does not contradict "other." The concrete has what it requires, and anything has what it requires, to be itself; but what the concrete requires and has is rich internal relatedness or relativity. Only the abstract can be independent of other things, even though it must be embodied in some concrete thing or other.

It seems possible to define relativity and nonrelativity in purely logical terms by employing Carnap's notion of "state descriptions," each of which is an ideally complete description of a cosmic state of affairs or a Leibnitzian possible world.[2] According to Carnap, there is one true state description valid for all time (as well as about all time) and this, for reasons the reader may surmise, I should not wish to endorse, but for the present purpose this issue may be waived. We define, then, as follows (probably in insufficiently precise language) : A is relative to B, or relation to B is internal to A, if and only if every state description affirming A also affirms B. Example: every state description affirming the existence of red apples must also affirm that of red things ; hence "red apple" is relative to "red thing." More generally, particulars are relative to the universals they instance. Negatively: A is not relative to B (is, in so far, absolute), or, relation to B is external to A, if and only if there is at least one state description affirming A and denying B. Example: "red thing" is not relative to "this red apple," for red thing can be affirmed of a world while apples of that color, not to mention this particular red apple, are not. More generally, universals are not relative to particulars instancing them.

2. "A class of sentences in [semantical system] S_1 which contains for every atomic sentence either this sentence or its negation, but not both, and no other sentences, is called a *state*-description in S_1, because it obviously gives a complete description of a possible state of the universe of individuals with respect to all properties and relations expressed by predicates of the system." *Meaning and Necessity: A Study in Semantics and Modal Logic* (The University of Chicago Press, 1946), 9.

It follows from the foregoing that every nonrelative or absolute factor must appear in more than one state description. Unless there are factors confined to a single state description, every factor is in some aspect nonrelative. In Carnap's conception, the total state description is itself entirely relative; for it seems there is no way in which it could be contained in any other state description, since in it all time is already accounted for. But anything short of the total state description must be capable of appearing in more than one SD (to abbreviate "state description"). It seems self-evident that the more universal a conception is the greater the range of state descriptions it can appear in. Thus "being" can be affirmed in every SD, unless total nonbeing is a conceivable state of affairs, and even if it is, being would be affirmed in every SD save one. So far, we seem to affirm nothing that can be denied by one who admits any distinction between necessary and contingent truths. It seems doubtful if logic can "possibly" get along without the idea of possibility, in the sense which implies pairs of alternatives neither of which is necessary; and such pairs must have at least some universals in common. From this it follows that there are alternative state descriptions in which universals play the role of more or less independent or nonrelative factors.

Difficulty arises only when we consider relations, not between universals and particulars, but between particulars as related in space-time, or in the manner of subject-object. Assuming that, while only one state description is true (at a given time, at any rate) others are nevertheless conceivable, we face the following principal alternatives. A) The untrue SD's have in common with the true only abstract universals, but no particulars, no determinate events. This would mean that a single momentary experience, say, would be internally related to every particular that is or ever could be in the actual universe. B) The untrue SD's and the true one have particulars in common, in such fashion that a possible world and the actual one may have the same past (down to a given moment) yet a different future, but not conversely. C) They may have the same future and a different past, but not conversely. D) They may have either the same past and a different future, or the same future and a different past. According to A, every particular is such that its complete description entails that of every other actual particular; according to B, later particulars thus entail earlier, but not conversely; according to C, earlier entail later, but not conversely; according to D, there is entailment neither way. The implication of A is that possibility is significant only because of our ignorance, since if we knew enough we should not distinguish between what happens and what might happen; we should simply recognize the actual course of the world throughout all time. That other worlds were possible would not be a truth descriptive of *this* world, since relations within this world would be free from alternatives, determinate in both temporal directions. I believe that sufficient reflection will find this result a *reductio ad absurdum*. It makes alternative possibilities irrelevant to actuality. What at any time in the past, however remote, could have been known as false is not significantly "possible." The implication of D is that relations between earlier and later do not form part of any particular event, but are at no time. This, too, I believe cannot stand careful analysis. We are left with B and C.

Let us consider the case in which an event is known or referred to by a later event, the earlier being "object," and the later subject. Thus Washington, as a stream of experiences occurring in the eighteenth century, is known by Truman, a stream of experiences occurring in the twentieth century. The knowing occurs in the latter century. When does the "being known" by Truman occur? Surely it also occurs in the twentieth century. In Washington's lifetime there was no such thing as being known by Truman, any more than such a thing as Truman knowing. If, then, we ascribe "being known by Truman" to Washington, it follows that this "property" belongs to Washington, not in the eighteenth but in the twentieth century! Thus the twentieth-century Truman possesses the subject-object relation in the twentieth century, but the eighteenth-century Washington fails to possess the converse relation in the eighteenth century. I suggest that this is an indication not to be taken lightly that the converse relation really does not constitute a property of the eighteenth-century occurrences called Washington. Thus, as between B and C, we have reason to prefer B. And the example illustrates at once both the nonrelativity of earlier to later and of object to subject, as well as the relativity of later to earlier and of subject to object.

It may be objected that the foregoing discussion is on the level of vague common-sense conceptions, rather than that of exact knowledge such as is achieved in physics. In terms of physical laws, with their approximate or statistical character, neither past nor future particulars are precisely implicated in present fact, so far as knowable. To this objection the reply must be that although physics is more exact than common-sense knowledge, it attains this superior exactitude at the price of a certain abstractness, and that it is the "fallacy of misplaced concreteness" to identify what is knowable in this manner with the real or knowable as such. Peirce, Whitehead, James, Bergson, and others have, I think, shown that this identification is inadmissible. It is not by technical physics that we learn what "past" as such means, but by the intuitive data of memory, in contrast with those of anticipation and present perception; just as (cf. the many discussions of this topic in Whitehead) it is not by physics that we know what "causal efficacy" or causal order, as such, are. Only the particular details of causation are (approximately) revealed by physics; the basic principles of cosmic coherence are given to the very animals in their emotional-practical experience.

It might be objected also that though "known by Truman" was not a predicate of the eighteenth-century Washington, "to be known by Truman" may have been such a predicate. But either "known by Truman" is included in or entailed by "to be known by Truman," or it is not. If it is, then we have the paradox that a complex predicate exists (or is actualized) when its constituent does not. If it is not entailed (and in that case, what does the expression mean?), then the implication remains that "known by Truman" is not a constituent or property of the eighteenth-century phenomenon.

A seemingly comparable argument has often been used to prove that the past cannot be literally known in the present, since it does not exist in the present if it is really past. But this overlooks the cumulative or incremental nature of time. If X is an ingredient present in memory-of-X, this does not abolish the distinction between memory-of-X, which is the present, and X, which is its past ingredient within it. Memory of X is logically richer than X alone—so far as the memory is not diluted with forgetting. The past is distinguished by its logical meagerness and the nonrelativity which goes with this. But if X contained an ideally complete anticipation of memory-of-X, then there would be no gain in richness when the memory became actual.

Could a state description affirming a man with the characteristics (known to us or not) of the actual Washington as an eighteenth-century phenomenon deny that there is a man corresponding to Truman? If among the characteristics of Washington must be included, "was, much later, followed in the presidency by Truman," then the reply must be in the negative. The question thus becomes whether or not "was followed by Truman" genuinely describes Washington. We must here distinguish between "wholly (or irreducibly) genuine" and "partly (or reducibly) genuine" descriptions (using this term very generally to mean any statement of what an entity is, not in the special sense of Russell's theory of descriptions). A description is partly genuine if some but not all of its implications are genuine. Thus "was followed in the presidency by Truman" (which we may call description D) implies that Washington was a president, and it would scarcely be denied that this, so far as it goes, does describe Washington, tells us what, at one period of his life, he was. But "followed by Truman" is another matter. No doubt any distinct and accurate grasp of Truman's state of mind during his presidency would find that this involves some image of or reference to Washington. But Washington's presidency, as a state of *his* mind, seems, according to all our knowledge, to have involved no image of Truman. If so, D is a reducible or not wholly genuine description of Washington. Again, "Jefferson disliked Hamilton" seems to convey something about the quality of Jefferson which could not wholly be expressed without reference to Hamilton; but by contrast, "T. V. Smith in the twentieth century likes Jefferson" seems (so far as Jefferson is concerned) only a way of saying that he had certain qualities, which could be described without mention of the twentieth-century admirer. Minds, as knowers, must somehow contain reference, relation, to their objects, or they are not knowers and (at the limit) not minds; but the entities which certain minds know and call their objects need not have this status in themselves. As we have seen, anything can be an "object." Hence "object" is not a description of one thing rather than another. Columbus was a certain sort of man, whether or not Washington later thought about him. A certain mathematician is such in that he sometimes thinks of numbers; but are numbers numbers in that this mathematician thinks of them? Would they not be just as much numbers were there not such a mathematician? Is there any relation between numbers which could not be exemplified in a possible world that did not involve the personal quality of feeling of this mathematician? So "relations between numbers" is nonrelative with regard to such personal qualities. We do not expect any study of arithmetic to tell us which part of the theory of numbers corresponds to our bank account; but we expect our bank account to mention certain numbers. If we wish to know whether or not George Santayana at five o'clock meditates upon "pure being," we do not ourselves meditate upon pure being (whether this be a concept or essence or what you will); we cable Santayana, "A penny for your five o'clock thoughts!" So it is the particular and the subject, not the universal or the object, that holds the secret of the relations of particular and universal, or subject and object. What can this mean if not that the particular and the subject are relative in a sense in which the universal and the object are not?

I do not know how much can be done to define the intuitive distinction between genuine and nongenuine relational descriptions. Perhaps it is about as clear as anything that could be used to define it. If "being-thought-of-by-X" is a genuine description of anything, then, since abstract entities are thought of, the full account of what "being in general," say, is, would include the most determinate concrete facts of psychology. And if "embodied in concrete entity C" is a genuine irreducible description of a universal, such as color, then the full account of what any universal is would be the full account of concrete things exemplifying it, and in the end the universal would be the concrete universe.

True, a number, or other abstraction or general factor, is in its very nature something which can be embodied in various things and which various minds can think about. But this, as we have seen, is no definite relation to any particular thing or mind, but only an indefinite relation to things or minds in general. This indefiniteness of relatedness defines what is meant by a universal, and by its abstractness. If one argues, as Blanshard, for example, does, that we can define a thing to be indefinite or abstractly universal without anything's really being so, the question is, does not he who says this presuppose "anything," "being," "definition," as real universals abstract in the sense in question. Similarly, he who says it is only for certain purposes that relations are nonessential presupposes that we can identify such a purpose without committing ourselves to all its future realizations. The very notion of a purpose is of something general, to which any fulfillment will be a genuine addition related to it as instance to universal. Otherwise purpose would be its fulfillment, the distinction would vanish, and with it anything we could mean by purpose.

Were there not objective indefiniteness, "real vagues" (Peirce), there would be nothing but an utterly unanalyzable ineffable something-everything-equals-nothing. Analysis and change and contingency and diversity would not be possible.

The definitions of relativity in terms of "state descriptions" and in terms of "wholly genuine" descriptions are inverse to each other, as follows. If there is *any* wholly genuine description of A which entails every genuine description of B, then and only then A is relative to B; but this means that *every* state description affirming A also affirms B. If there is *no* wholly genuine description of A entailing every genuine description of B, then and only then is A nonrelative to B; but this means that at least *some* state description affirms A and denies B.

The axiom of logic that "every relation has a converse," so that if A is related to B, B must be related to A, according to our argument is subject to the qualification that the converse may in some cases be vacuous—not internally or genuinely or irreducibly descriptive. One reason that this has not been seen, I think, is that almost any, if not quite any, namable relation will in some sense have a genuine converse. Thus being-known is genuine if it merely means that the entity is known to some mind; for, just as it may be held that the abstract must be "embodied" in *some* concrete case or other, so it may be held that any entity must be known by some subject or other, even though being known by any particular subject is external to the entity. Also being known by X is genuine, or at least is part of a relation that is genuine, if the known is a person aware that he is known. The same is true of "predecessor." Or again, in an abstract schema of time laid down in advance, as in a calendar, it is as true of June first that it precedes June second as conversely.

And many of the relations most interesting to logicians are apparently equally genuine whether they are read from A to B or from B to A. Thus if A is greater than B, where both are abstract magnitudes, then it seems just as descriptive to say that B is less than A. Yet a vacuous case of greater than is indeed possible: "a certain house, no longer existent, was smaller than this newly-built house." This ascribes a size to the former house, but that size could be more exactly specified without mention of the later house, by giving the dimensions in feet or meters. So the relational element is not wholly or irreducibly genuine. It is different if one man consciously surpasses or is inferior to another in size or otherwise. Here being greater or less than is a genuine relation. For understandable reasons, logicians have not been interested in such distinctions.[3]

3. Concerning the metaphysics of relations, see: A. C. Ewing, *Idealism* (London, 1934), chap. iv; DeW. H. Parker, *Experience and Substance* (Ann Arbor, 1941), chaps. x–xi; Brand Blanshard, *The Nature of Thought* (London, 1939), chaps. xxxi–xxxii; A. N. Whitehead, *Science and the Modern World* (New York, 1925), pp. 174 f., 223; also *Adventures of Ideas* (1933), p. 201. Concerning Blanshard's skillful attempt to show that all relations are internal to all their terms, I remark that much of its force depends on attacking the thesis of external relations as applied to terms to which, according to Surrelativism also, it is inapplicable, such as effects in relation to causes, or abstractions in relation to others of the same or higher generality, or knowledge in relation to the known.

To ask, is God supremely relative, is to ask, is there any wholly genuine description of him which entails every genuine description of the actual universe? Yes, indeed, if it is genuinely descriptive of him to say that God infallibly knows that that universe exists. Defective knowledge may indeed be neutral to relational alternatives, and this is exactly its defect, that it fails faithfully to define, through its own actuality, the relational pattern of things. Furthermore, by the test, "Which term in the relation is it whose nature is consulted in order to learn if the relation obtains?" God, as generally conceived, must be a relative term in his cognition of the world. For theologians have nearly all told us that God knows the world by intuiting his own actuality. It follows logically that this actuality cannot be neutral to relational alternatives. And the argument, once more, is unaffected by the assumption that the divine knowing does, or does not, create its objects. In order to establish for the divine intuition which possible relations are actual, or are created—it matters not, in this context, how we put it—the divine nature which is intuited must depart from relational neutrality, by every definition or test we have been able to find.

A possible objection to the criterion of relativity furnished by the question, "which term is it whose nature is consulted to ascertain the relation?" is as follows. A wire, we believe, really contains an electric charge, "moving electrons." But we do not observe this electronic structure by inspecting the wire, but by inspecting what happens to a light attached to the wire, or some other effect beyond the wire itself. Thus the locus where something is observed may be different from where it is. I reply, either an observation of the charge in the wire itself is in principle possible, if not for man then for some other mind; or, if this be false, then the electric charge must *be* a relation between the wire and the light, and furthermore a relation which not the wire but only the light genuinely possesses. I should hold the first alternative, that some mind, no doubt necessarily other than human (for our direct intuitions are chiefly of our own bodies and our own psychical past) can directly intuit the electrons in the wire. At least God, on my view, does so. What not even God could do, for it is meaningless, is to intuit, as constitutional of being-as-such, that there is a certain man thinking of being. Any "being" which thus involves a concrete subject (or stream of subjects) would not be being as such, being as a general.

It is less obvious, but, I hold, still manifest to careful consideration, that not even God himself could intuit in the earthly actuality of George Washington that Truman thinks of Washington. For this would dovetail later into earlier events, and then nothing would really be earlier or later. Also, once more, we note that determinate subject-object relations are found in subjects, not in objects. Subjectivity as such is relativity, objectivity as such is nonrelativity. And if it be objected that "objectivity as such" manifestly involves relation, the relation of being known, the reply, once more, is that this is a "determinable" relation to mind as such and in general, not a determinate relation to any given mind or set of minds, even the cosmic set. The object can be object if *any* mind, some mind or other, knows it; but the subject is an ignorant subject, deficient as such (at the limit nonexistent) in so far as it is nonrelative or neutral to the question, *which* objects, of those that might exist, do exist?

That knowing includes relation to the known has been obscured from some philosophers by a curious semantic confusion. It has been argued that knowledge must "transcend" itself, get "outside" itself, to know an independent and larger world. If the known is outside the knower, then relation-to-the-known must, at least partly, fall outside the knower. The semantic confusion here is a double one: first, it is argued that the object must be independent of the subject, therefore (*sic*) external to the subject. But independent of is logically one thing, external to, quite another. Has it been proved that every sort of whole must act upon all its parts to deprive them of independence? Is every whole entirely "organic" in this sense? The very people who use this argument are, so far as I know, the last to maintain such an extreme of "organicism." Then what does the argument amount to? The second confusion is in supposing that since the world we seek to know is a larger one, and in so far is not embraced in ourselves, this must be true even of that much of the world that we do know. But this too is a non sequitur. If we knew the world in such fashion that there was nothing of it that we did not adequately know, would it still seem to us larger than and partly outside of ourselves? I know of no valid reason for supposing this. The vaunted transcendence, taken as externality of known to knower, is thus really a defect of our human knowledge. Since it is, quantitatively, incomparably more true that we do not know the world than that we do know it, our impression that the world stretches vastly beyond us is only what we should expect.

It seems likely that one reason for the view that mind does not literally include its objects, or that (as the scholastics say) "intensional inherence" is not "entitative" or literal inherence, is the fact that we can mean what does not exist. We can mean fairies without containing any. As an explicit argument this seems too fallacious to have influenced any good reasoner, but it may have had some sort of subliminal effect. We do not literally have fairies when we think of them, but the reason is that what we think of are only complexes of qualities, more or less abstract and vague, plus possibly the abstract notion, there may or might be such things. Now the complexes of qualities which we really are aware of do exist in some fashion in our minds, even though individual fairies, concrete fairies, do not exist there or anywhere else. Concrete things are only in a very qualified sense objects of our human awareness. Another argument, used in the Middle Ages, and also more recently, is this: we can mean past or future events, and these do not exist in present awareness. Our doctrine answers as follows. Future events are a mere intensional class without extension, and only as such can they be intended without absurdity. There is no logical path from, "we can mean what is not actual in our minds," to "we can mean what is actual outside our minds." As for past events, these indeed have the mode of actuality, yet not of the latest actuality, the present. The object, I have held, so far as object, is within us—for relation-to-O includes O. But if O is a past event, it has not always been within this present knowledge, K. When O was, not past, but present, it was not in K at all. So, though it is now in K, or rather K now includes it (for "in" here is not a genuine relation), K did not always do so. Not that previously O was "outside" K, for then there was no K to be outside of. First there is O—period. Then there is K-including-O. This is what becoming is, the actualization of new terms related, whose relata include old terms independent of the new relations. Since the past includes all abstract factors of being, the independence of such factors is thus also provided for. May we not conclude that the identification of "independent object" and "external object" is a confusion of meanings? It is the subject that is "outside" the object, as it were surrounding but not penetrating it.

If one wants an image for the coming to be of an external relation, it is not too difficult to form one. Imagine an envelope to form around an entity without there being any change or reaction of the entity. One may then verbally say that the entity has passed from the state of not "being surrounded" to that of being surrounded; but according to our hypothesis (which could even be so formulated as not to violate any known physical laws) this is a vacuous manner of speaking, since there has been no change in the entity to represent this coming to be surrounded. But suppose (and here we may get into trouble with assumed physical laws) the envelope contains within itself reference to what it surrounds, say if it is conscious of the surrounding. Then this relation is a real property of the envelope, descriptive of it but not of the original entity. True, the description of the envelope E includes that of the original entity O, but the converse does not hold. O is used (rather, we use it) to describe E, but not E to describe O. The description is *about* O but not *of* O, and this distinction is not merely grammatical. For, suppose that a complete description of any one thing must include all relations of other terms to the thing. Then contingency could have no meaning, for even the most abstract entities must have been different if anything had been different. Being must have "been" other than being, truth other than truth, etc. That way nonsense lies.

Let us consider the logical relation of entailment. If P entails Q, it need not be that Q entails P. But suppose that being-entailed is a genuine property. Then, since blue entails colored, being-entailed-by-blue is a property of colored. The result would be that the simplest most abstract factors must have all the complexity of the most specific or concrete, and that the entailed in a sense always entails its entailer. For a thing entails what it is, and if Q *is* something "entailed by P," then it entails P as a factor in itself as relational. Some would think this is not a reduction to absurdity, for they would say, is not the genus the disjunctive set of its species? It entails them, but only as alternative possibilities, not as actualities. Yes, but the actual species entails the genus, and hence, on the hypothesis, the genus is entailed-by the actual species. Further, the genus is not a disjunctive set of species, nor is the species a disjunctive set of individuals. This, I hold, is an impossible extreme of nominalism. It abolishes any clear difference between possible and actual, or determinable and determinate, or intension and extension.

It seems we must choose: either the full account of what each thing is would entail that of every other thing, or it would not. If it would, then it is only our ignorance that makes us think that certain relations are additions to certain terms, that makes us think there are real generals (that is to say, entities which may be involved in "instances" but do not involve these instances), that there are real contingencies, alternatives of being to which being is neutral or nonrelative. In this case (but there is, on the assumption, no meaning to "case," for there are no universals and no alternatives), thought can only bow itself out in favor of the mystic silence. Alas, those so "thinking" do not cease to talk!

It is sometimes said that the theory of internal relations destroys the difference between qualities and relations, or between nonrelational and relational predicates, one-place and several-place predicates. But in assigning to X as its internal property relation-to-Y we do not deny the twoness of X and Y. We say only that X is inclusive of the other entity. If X includes Y, they remain none the less two entities. The Aristotelian theory of substances as mutually exclusive, as subjects that cannot be predicates, has much to answer for here. "Fond of Shakespeare" is a predicate which includes an individual, and whatever has this predicate has Shakespeare. Thus individuals can and must be predicated. The psychological reason for the contrary view can be imagined with some plausibility. Our experience is extremely vague or faint in most of its intuitions of predicates, and hence of the individuals included in some of these. This faintness and vagueness make it easy to fancy that no such concrete rich entity as Shakespeare can be in the intuited predicates. Certainly the richness is not *effectively* intuited, is not introspectively distinct and unmistakable. If it were, we should be the divine intuition.

In this regard Bradley may be accused of the error he most

sought to avoid, anthropomorphism. He contends that the relationless unity of what he chooses to call the absolute may best be interpreted by analogy with the unity of feeling in our immediate experience. True it is that in human experience direct feeling does not exhibit individuals as such with much distinctness. But why does it not? To exhibit adequately other individuals our experience and our individuality would have to be effectively inclusive of their value. Then we should be their superiors, for we should have in addition whatever was distinctive of ourselves. When we recall the esthetic law that the more an artistic unity can permit rich individuation of its members, the higher the unity (thus drama is superior to an oriental rug), we can hardly doubt that the "relationless unity," i.e., the absence of effective individuation providing conspicuous terms for relations, characterizing our direct experience is a human limitation which we should hesitate to attribute to the superhuman or highest. In order to plainly exhibit full-fledged individuals and their relations in his experience, deity must be radically the superior of all individuals other than himself. But such superiority is just what Bradley claimed to be looking for!

Theoretically, we might indeed have fairly distinct intuitions of subhuman individuals. But the question arises, Would this be suitable to our needs? Such individuals are not individually important to us. What is important in their regard is either the behavior of masses of individuals, such as those composing our bodies, or the behavior of single animals other than human in terms of generic more than of individual traits.

CHAPTER III

The Divine Attributes as Types of Social Relationship

Failure of the Historical Doctrines

WHAT troubles theologians have had with the "attributes" of God! God, it seems, has all-power, absolute power. Does this mean that, since he has all the power, we have none; or that, since he does or can do everything, we do or need do nothing? And when we sin against God, does God himself "do" this? Of course (we are told), not exactly. Man has free will, and secondary causes are real as well as the primary cause. But what then *is* meant by all-powerful? Again, God, it seems, has perfect knowledge. Does this mean that all things are objects of cognitive relations, with God as their subject, thus relativizing him with respect to all things whatsoever? If, on the contrary, as was generally maintained, the divine knowledge is purely absolute, hence involves no relation to things known, what analogy can it have to what is commonly meant by knowledge, which seems to be nothing without such a relation? Ah, you see, runs the reply, God knows things through his own all-causative essence, and, therefore, his cognitive relation is self-relation, and implies no relativity. Yes, but "causative" seems to mean related to effects. And either a cognitive relation is established, not just to the cause but also to the effects, or these are not known. Also, we are told that God's knowledge *is* his essence —and indeed, if there are no contingent or inessential properties in God, it must be his essence. If, then, knowledge that John exists is in God's essence, then, since John is essential to knowledge-that-John-exists, John, a contingent being, must be required by the essence of God! No, not exactly. How then?

Consider the following argument:

1. What a necessary premise implies has the same necessity as the premise itself (self-evident principle of logic).

2. "God knows that men exist" implies "men exist" (self-evident, assuming that he "knows" infallibly).

3. No property of God, nothing in God, could be otherwise, the whole nature of God is unconditionally necessary (traditional theological doctrine).

Conclusion: either the designatum of "God knows that men exist" is in God as something unconditionally necessary—and then (by 1 and 2), "men exist" is also unconditionally necessary, has the same necessity as the nature of God—or "God knows that men exist" does not describe anything in God.

I have discussed this repeatedly with defenders of orthodoxy. The argument proves, in my opinion, that one of these three must be true: (1) there is nothing whose existence is in any sense contingent; all things are necessary in the same sense; (2) God does not know the contingent as existent; or finally (3) there are contingent properties in God. This last is of course the solution accepted by surrelativism. It is the only way to combine, without contradiction, the assertions: God knows all truth, and, not all truths are necessary.

Let us consider again the contention that, since God's essence is cause of all things (though not related to them), the divine self-knowledge must include knowledge of all that can be caused by the essence. Note that what can be caused by the essence is, in so far, merely a possible world; it is actual only if it not only can be, but is, caused by the es-

sence. Now the actually being-caused of this world is either
in the essence or it is not. If it is, then to know the essence
is to know the actuality of this world; but on pain of this
actuality's having the same necessity as the essence itself.
If it is not in the essence, then God may have all the self-
knowledge you please, he still (if there is nothing in himself
but his essence) will not thereby know which, among the
worlds he might create, he does create. When they permit
themselves to become aware of this difficulty, theologians
now and then change the tune by remarking that to know
the actual, as distinct from the possible, God must indeed
inspect something besides his essence as object of his "understanding"; he must take note, as it were, of the decision
of his "will." That is, he must answer the question, what
world do I decide to create by means of my essence? Yes,
but we are blandly told, "his will is his essence." So we are
off on the same contradictory circuit. How can a free decision among possibilities be a necessary essence? (It can
very well be the divine essence to make *some* free decision or
other. Choosing-as-such can itself be necessary, not free.
But it is quite another thing to say that the particular use
of the freedom, any given choice, is itself essential or necessary. That would be self-contradictory.) Suppose, on the
other hand, it be denied that the divine decision to create
this world is in the essence of God. Where then is it? We
must choose: the decision is (1) in the essence, and then it
is necessary, not free (without "liberty to act or refrain
from acting"), (2) it is in God, but not in his essence (i.e.,
as something contingent—the surrelativistic solution), or
(3) it is not in God at all. What, on the last view, is an act
of will not in the agent said to be willing?

Such are the paradoxes in the view I combat. Cognition
implies the reality of what is known to be real, but in application to God that which logically results from this self-

evident axiom is denied. Decision essentially implies the possibility of an alternative act as an alternative state of the agent; but in God nothing in any way analogous to this is admitted to be possible—yet there is in him something analogous to decision! If the reader feels these criticisms must be unfair, he has only to consult the correspondence between Leibnitz and Arnauld to find the virtual admission, by both of these high authorities, that the orthodox view does involve the contradictions I allege, and that nothing can be done to remove them, within the assumptions of that view.[1]

To be sure, it is explained that properties are not attributable to God and the creatures univocally, in the same sense. Yet neither, it is contended, are they merely equivocal. Maimonides and Spinoza, saying that God and man have understanding in common somewhat as a dog star is a dog, were frowned upon as extremists. They seemed to be saying that theology is a sophisticated way of telling lies to the pious. Nevertheless, the line between equivocal meanings and the so-called "analogical" ones is not so well-drawn in orthodox systems that it can be seen at all by most of us who are not adherents of such systems. To call "knowledge" what, in one case, means a constitutive cognitive relation of knowing and a nonconstitutive relation of being known, and in the other case, a nonconstitutive relation of knowing and a constitutive one of being known, looks to some of us, to speak frankly, like the merest deception, the merest intellectual fraud, however pious or well-intentioned or unconscious. Everything that we know about knowledge and about logic is gone if it be not true that "knowing such and such exists" implies "it does exist," or if a premise can be "independent" of its implied conclusion. If this is the best

1. *Discourse on Metaphysics* (Open Court ed.), Letters vi, viii, pp. 96, 114–115.

that theism can do, its case is precarious indeed. For two thousand years, men have sought to avoid a decision between defining God in terms of eminence, under various categories, and defining him merely in terms of the assertion or denial of these categories. Confusion was the inevitable result. Eminence is not identical with nonrelative, for eminent relativity can as easily be defined as eminent absoluteness; it is not identical with nonmutable, for eminent mutability is as definable as eminent permanence or stability; it is not identical with simplicity or noncompositeness, for an eminent manner of composition is as definable as an eminent lack of composition; it is not identical with nonpassive, for eminent passivity is as definable as eminent activity. And in all these cases the definitions that really make sense imply no contradiction in the attribution to the same being (in diverse aspects, now as abstract, now as concrete) of *both* eminent absoluteness and eminent relativity, eminent permanence and eminent change; eminent simplicity and eminent complexity, eminent activity and eminent passivity. The divine is to be conceived as relative beyond all other relative things, but this relativity itself must have an abstract character which is fixed or absolute. Let us see how this doctrine enables us to construct a consistent theory of divine attributes.

Contemplative Adequacy or Omniscience

It will be admitted that though concrete things may perhaps, in spite of Plato, be "equal" to each other, equality itself is an abstraction. The notion of ideal knowledge or omniscience is similarly abstract. Omniscience is knowledge that is in some sense equal to its objects, whereas nonomniscience is knowledge unequal to what it knows. For example, the subtlety of nature, as Bacon said, surpasses radically the subtlety of our human perceptions and ideas. The di-

vine subtlety must be at least equal to that of its objects.
Let us call this "at-least-equal" relation, the relation of
"adequacy." But note that it is really a type of relation, not
a relation. The adequacy of a knower to object O is not the
same relation as the adequacy of a knower to object O
prime. The two relations are of the same type; but still they
are diverse relations. It may seem that adequate knowledge,
being knowledge of all things, would be constituted by a
single inclusive and unique relation, since its term is the
one totality of being. But in what sense can being form a
total? We must remember that there are actualities, and
also potentialities which are capable of actualization. Suppose some of the potentialities actualized (for that they can
be actualized is what is meant by calling them potentialities) ; then we have a new totality of actualized being,
compared to that which obtained, or would obtain, prior to,
or without, the actualization. Knowledge adequate to its
objects must be knowledge of the actual as actual and of the
possible as possible. Accordingly, for every possible total of
actuality there is a distinct possible relation of adequate
knowledge to that possible totality. Thus omniscience is an
infinite class of relationships, not all of which are actual.
The common property which generates or describes this
class is the relational type, "cognitive adequacy." But the
type of a relation is not itself subject to the relation, is not
relativized by it. "Greater than" is not itself greater than,
cognitive adequacy does not itself know, whether adequately or otherwise—any more than it is volition that wills.
It is the man who wills. We must learn to avoid passing back
and forth from abstract to concrete in theology, without
taking note of the passage and its logical consequences. If
volition does not will, and cognitive adequacy does not
know, then cognitive adequacy need not be relative, even
though the adequate knower himself is relative, relative to

what he knows. Thus there is in God something absolute or nonrelative, his cognitive adequacy. Nevertheless, in knowing any actual thing, God himself is related and relativized with respect to that thing. There is here no paradox, unless it be paradoxical that seeing does not see, or that humor does not laugh.

It may be objected that such abstractions as humor do not really exist, but are mere conceptions. I reply that even if one takes the "conceptualist" solution of the problem of nominalism and realism, one need not therefore deny that God may have something corresponding to concepts, and hence, granting that "adequacy" as such is of the nature of a concept, such a concept may still be an essential factor in the being of God. The content or meaning of the concept is absolute in a strict sense. He who conceives adequacy, as such, does not thereby conceive the adequacy of just this knowing to just that (contingent) object. He precisely does not conceive any given case of adequacy, but adequacy solely as such and in general. This conception is absolute, so far as any particular case is concerned.

We have seen how absoluteness or neutrality to relational alternatives permits degrees as well as an eminent case, so that certain things are independent with respect to some but not all relations permitting such independence. We have seen, further, that relativity likewise permits degrees and an eminent case, the surrelative or supreme subject. We have now to note that relatedness admits intensive, and not just numerical or extensive, gradations. Thus the relation of knowing has gradations of clearness as well as of scope. I and some great mathematician both know the number one hundred. But the mathematician knows it much more clearly. Or I may myself remember the same past event several times, now very unclearly, now with comparative clearness. Why may not God's act of knowing all things relate him, and, let us be frank, relativize him with respect to all things with an *adequacy* compared to which our own cognitive relatedness is almost equivalent to non-relationship? We are cognitively related *effectively* to but a tiny fragment of the world. If God is not cognitively related effectively to the whole world, then surely nothing has such eminent relatedness! All our experience supports the view that cognitive relativity is a merit and possession, not a weakness or defect. Why should we refuse to attribute an eminent form of this relativity to God? There is but one reason: the prejudice that God must be absolute, not simply in some intelligible sense, but in every sense, intelligible or otherwise.

In fairness, it ought to be admitted that there seemed a good reason for traditional procedure in regard to the divine knowing. Must not God's knowledge create the world, hence must not our being-known by him be a constitutive relation? I reply that there is an escape from the apparent dilemma. God enables us to be by knowing us, but let us not forget that we too have knowledge, and that if we are able to know that God's knowledge creates us, this can only mean that his knowing us at least can be our object, our something known, hence constitutive of us as knowing. Objects are constitutive of subjects, even when the object or something known is another subject's knowledge of the first subject. Thus God perhaps creates us by knowing us only in that, otherwise, we could not have as object, as something known by us, his knowledge of us. There are reasons for thinking that subjects cannot exist except by including among the things they know a knowledge of themselves as possessed by other subjects. This is the social structure of subjectivity. God is important to us not simply because he knows us, or simply because we know him, but because we know or feel him as, with unique adequacy, knowing us.

The innermost secret of existence, it may be, is that the existence of anything other than God consists of its enjoyed contribution to the divine awareness. As mere object for the divine subjects, we should be nonentity, for nothing is mere object—since being-known is not a constitutive relation. But as objects which *enjoy* this status, which in some manner have their own being-object as itself their object, we may very well derive our whole being from this enjoyed being-object. Since any object is constitutive of the knower, then one's own being-known, so far as one knows this, is constitutive. True, this would not explain how creatures which are not subjects, or composed of subjects or abstract features of subjects, could depend upon God. But it will be time to consider this question when someone can show, against most great modern philosophers, that there are any such creatures, any such "vacuous" actualities, void of enjoyment.

The upshot of the foregoing is that the dependence of lesser subjects upon the divine knower does not mean a reversal of the subject-object relativity. Therewith falls the last excuse for this reversal, this lapse from realism. It is open to us to adopt a sweeping and consistent program of attributing to God the supereminent form of every property capable of such a form. Thus the theological analogies can at last be free of arbitrariness and contradiction.

Motivational Adequacy or Holiness

In human beings, knowing is one thing, doing another. Yet, in principle, it is correct that virtue is knowledge. To know the good is to value it; for it is to know the intrinsically satisfying, that which one can only be aware of by rejoicing in it. There is no reason or motive for pursuing the good but the good itself. To know the end is to have all the motive there can be for seeking to actualize it. If, then, God is adequately aware of all actuality as actual and all possibility as possible, he has adequate motivation for seeking to actualize maximal possibilities of further value. There can be no ethical appeal beyond the decision of the one who in his decision takes account of all actuality and possibility. To what could the appeal be made? Not to some ethical "principle." For a principle cannot be anything beyond actuality and possibility. It is idle to say that God ought to respond to the greater values among those he is aware of. To be aware of their greatness is to respond to them, and this awareness is no addition to adequate knowing. We could only criticize God's decisions on the basis of our ignorance, for so far as we know, we must agree with God as to the values of things. Ethical rules are substitutes for adequate awareness by which we guard against the more dangerous effects of our ignorance. Dewey is theologically right, though humanistically somewhat misleading, in arguing that the basis of ethical decision is the total, unique, concrete situation, not some abstract rule. The only difficulty is that man does not see the concrete situation, except with enormous and more or less wilfully selected blind spots. Hence he needs the help of rules, adopted in moments of calm and disinterested reflection, to protect himself and others against the bias of his perceptions and inferences. But God needs nothing but his perceptive grasp of the actual and potential experiences and interests, and the power of reaching a decision, any decision, taking account of what he perceives. There could not be a wrong decision which thus took account of the situation; for a right decision can be defined as one adequately informed as to its context. Omniscience in action is by definition right action. Nor is this definition merely arbitrary. Selfish, wicked men do not, in the moments of actual decision, face the actual and potential factors to which the decision relates.

They invariably deceive themselves in some essential way as
to what they are doing and what they are dealing with and
what it is possible for them to do. The reason that in us
knowledge is not identical with virtue is only that we mean
by knowing not necessarily the actual, concrete awareness
of things, but the virtual or abstract awareness of them.
Thus a man may know that his acts will have harmful consequences in the sense that, if asked, he would give the right
answer to questions; but it does not follow that in the precise moment of decision he has these matters present to his
mind with any concreteness and correctness. However, the
divine or adequate awareness cannot in this way escape the
identity of knowing and valuing. While virtual and abstract knowledge has little of the values of concrete reality,
actual and concrete knowledge has all the values, and cannot fail to respond; for the ability to be aware and the
ability to respond are identical. One can only be aware in
responding. Ultimately knowing and deciding are mutually
inseparable. Even in us they are inseparable; but our inadequate knowledge is also inadequate response and may
lead to the choice of even less adequate response; but where
knowledge cannot be inadequate, such inadequacy cannot
be chosen, and response likewise can only be adequate.

Although the mere awareness of actual and possible
values constitutes of itself the correct evaluation of them,
it is possible to abstract some general features of this evaluation. What are these general features or "principles" embodied in the divine goodness of purpose? It is an old query:
is not God's goodness so far above ours that to us it may
appear evil? Thus God seems frequently to reward the
righteous with suffering and premature death and the
wicked with long life and prosperity, whereas even a human
judge will seek to make the punishment or reward fit the
crime or the desert. Whether, or in what sense, God is

cause of all things, including suffering, will be considered when we discuss God's power. Meanwhile, it is perhaps necessary to say that human wisdom and goodness are not exhausted or even primarily illustrated in a judge, taken merely as dispensing punishments and rewards. There are two basic ways in which we may hope that human beings will be induced to act helpfully and constructively toward one another. One is that they will learn to love one another and wish well to one another as intrinsically valuable. The other is that they will be led by rewards and punishments to act toward others somewhat as they would act if they wished them well; but for the very different reason that they wish well merely to themselves, with reference to future rewards and punishments to be visited upon them. Now it is not necessarily divine wisdom but may be ordinary, human, ethical insight to see that the second of these ways of "social control" is radically inferior to the first, a poor second best, to be resorted to only so far as the first fails. Yet what have theologians said as to God? That for his dealing with us, the second way is an ultimate good in itself, since it is the preservation of the divine majesty by the punishment of evildoers or rebellious subjects and the confirmation of goodness by its future rewarding. But a man who does good to others because he wishes good to them, if that is really his motive, needs no future reward for himself, and any such is irrelevant. The influence of the self-interest theory of motivation, derived partly from Aristotle (in whom it was partly corrected by the principle of political obligation), upon saints writing theological systems, forms a depressing subject.

The holiness of God consists, I dare to say, not in a strange reconciliation of justice and mercy, each somehow an ultimate principle of value, but in the single aim at the one primary good, which is that the creatures should enjoy rich harmonies of living, and pour this richness into the one ultimate receptacle of all achievement, the life of God. In certain cases this aim will be advanced by rewards and punishments, but only as a secondary device.

The word "justice" takes on so many meanings, and these shade into one another so subtly, that most of the arguments on this matter are semantic quagmires more than anything else. A "just man" really means something rather more and rather different from an efficient adjuster of rewards-punishment to desert. It means a man who will not cheat his friends to enrich himself or his mere acquaintances to enrich his friends. It is a matter of unselfishness and of adequate taking account, not primarily of the deserts of others, but of their needs and of the needs of men generally, including the need that certain things be done in certain customary and expected ways. The perpetual stress upon past deeds and accumulated merit or desert is not so much a fallacy of imputing human ways to God as it is an extremely narrow or false interpretation of human ways themselves.

A common objection to admitting that a God with an absolute character exists is that with this absolute are likely to go all sorts of others, such as absolute ethical codes or alleged divine commands. I wish to register a protest against the habit (which does not seem intellectually responsible and yet is frequent indeed) of vaguely lumping together all possible uses, good, bad, and indifferent, of the word absolute, and condemning all on the score of the bad. This is no more legitimate than a defense of all uses on the score of the good, and is not to be wholly excused even as a reaction against the latter practice. That God has an absolute goodness of purpose, in the sense analyzed above, lends no absolute "sanction" to anything else, certainly not to any human ethical code, however attributed to deity. For it is impossible that anything less than the eternal divine abstract purpose should be eternally valid, and this applies even to divine commands as specific concrete acts or decisions. They might be valid for all the future, but at least they could not have been for all the past. And how are we to know infallibly and accurately what God decrees? Human language itself, with its vagueness and ambiguities, seems enough to make this impossible. And these characters of human language form part of the general fallibility of human nature, which seems to refute any argument for an infallible revelation of God to man. Short of the "to man," the revelation may be as truly infallible as you please, but once it actually gets reception into human life the fallibility begins, and until it is thus received we know nothing about it. So it seems that to get rid of "vicious absolutes" there is no need whatever to get rid of the one thing that can, without vicious implications, be conceived absolute, the eternal adequacy of type in the divine relational acts, whose concrete characters are never clearly known to mere human beings. God himself is a supreme relativist, his absoluteness consisting in the ideally exhaustive way in which he relativizes his evaluations to all factors in the concrete actual world. This ideal relativity, absolute in its immutable adequacy, is the standard of all.

If the anthropologist can see how the needs and possible values in different societies over the earth vary, God can see it even better. The differences are (1) that God can also see that, though men differ among themselves, they also have a generic resemblance, as compared to monkeys and perhaps to inhabitants of planet Z; and (2) God can see, as anthropologists might not see, or not see so clearly, that while there are many ways of achieving a good human society, there are also ways of failing to achieve any very good form of social life; also, not all good social forms are necessarily equally good. Thus we might expect God to avoid a meaningless form of relativism which merely says: anything is good if someone likes it, and nothing is really better, for man as such, than anything else. We should not expect God to fall into the fallacy: polygamy is perhaps the least evil in a certain economic state of society, therefore a society whose economic state favors monogamy is merely different, but not better than the other. Since marriage is not merely an economic device, it might be worth rearranging the economic life, where possible, so as to remove the situation that made an inferior form of marriage (unequal status of men and women) the best form attainable in that situation. Experiences as such are the ultimate units of value, and these are good not because someone says so, but because anyone will say so in proportion as he adequately knows these experiences—as God alone fully knows them. A poem is in so far good if X richly enjoys it, but this enjoyment is appreciated by God (even though not perhaps by all philosophers and theologians) and thereby made an objective, i.e., permanent and cosmic, value.

The aim of creation, it has often been said, is to glorify God. Yes, but after all, does God need to be glorified? No, it was generally replied, he needs nothing. Does it in any way enhance the divine good to glorify it? In no way, for that good is in all respects incapable of enhancement. Why then is it important that God be glorified? Either there has been no answer, or the answer implied has been that it is important to man, and other creatures, for their own sakes, that God should be glorified—that is, in plain English, that God should be praised and made to seem as great as he would in any case be, even without glorification.

All the time that men were being told that their "end" was God, they were also being told, in effect, that it was of no importance to God that they attain this end, but only important to *them*. Thus essentially the end was humanly self-regarding—and in my opinion blasphemous. It made man, what he can never be, something ultimate. "Ultimate beneficiary" is no less an ultimate than ultimate benefactor, and man is not ultimate at all.

It may be replied that the Thomist doctrine is that the ultimate achieved good is neither man nor God, but the whole creation as end. Very well, let us argue it on that basis. Why or how is the created universe the ultimate beneficiary? This universe is either conscious or not conscious. We are not told it is conscious. If it is not, then the doctrine is that the ultimate recipient of intrinsic good is something unconscious. This defies the very meaning of good, which is satisfaction, fruition of purpose enjoyed by the purposer. On the other hand, if the universe is conscious, then it is either God or a God additional to God. If you say that the intrinsic value of the universe is in the divine consciousness for which it is object, then I reply that either you are saying, unclearly, what I am contending for, or you are indulging in equivocation. God either acquires value, and contingent value, from the contingent fact of creation, or he acquires no value. There is nothing between. Either God, or something other than God, is the ultimate or inclusive beneficiary of achievement. If God is the beneficiary, then it is wrong that God is cause but not effect of creativity. If the ultimate beneficiary is not God, then there are two ultimates, and really two Gods, since ultimacy is the privilege and meaning of deity.

Consider what happens to the problem of self-interest and altruism if one admits the idea of the divine as ultimate beneficiary of all acts. At a given moment, a man has to make a choice among several courses of action. He has to reject certain otherwise possible courses on the ground that they will be less likely to serve his ultimate purposes.

But what are his ultimate purposes? Are they to build a happy life for himself while on this earth? In that case no one should ever renounce his life in the interest of others, and a man should try not to consider what will happen to his family and to mankind after he dies. Indeed, a man should regard all sympathy for others as a response to be indulged only when it is likely to prove enjoyable. Such a man, if consistent, is not a man, but a monster. Again, is the ultimate purpose to build a happy life for oneself in heaven? Then everything depends upon whether there is a heaven, and what one's chances are of getting into it. Nothing else can, by comparison, have any value in our eyes, if this is our conception of life. Such a man, if consistent, is an even more impossible monstrosity than the previous. Berdyaev calls this the most disgusting morality ever conceived. And in addition, who really knows if there be a heaven to get into? Once more, is the ultimate purpose to build a happy life for men generally upon this earth? This presents two difficulties. In the long run, the likelihood seems to be that men generally will be neither happy nor unhappy, since all will be dead. This difficulty can be met by the dubious speculation of heaven or the dubious speculation that man will somehow learn to immortalize his kind in this precarious universe (the reason for this precariousness will be discussed in the next section) where suns eventually cool, perhaps after growing unbearably hot! But there is another difficulty. What does it mean to say, many men are happy, and their being happy is a good thing? That is good which is satisfying when and as experienced. But who is it who experiences the happiness of men in general? Each of us effectively enjoys only his own happiness, and something of that of a few around him. The sum of joys is not, it seems, itself a joy. How then is it a good, if the good be joy? And what else can it be?

The problem is solved if the general welfare of men (as at a given moment) is, as a whole, effectively enjoyed by a single subject in a single satisfying experience. Such a subject could not be less than divine. But the divine is here posited as beneficiary or recipient of created values. Granted this view, a man's ultimate purpose can at last be intelligibly stated. Old phrases can be used, but with a new singleness of meaning. The purpose is to serve and glorify God, that is, literally to contribute some value to the divine life which it otherwise would not have. Altruism toward God would include and embrace and unify all altruism. What then of self-interest? It would be preserved in its legitimate, and inhibited in its illegitimate, aspects. First, the man in the moment of choosing to serve God would himself enjoy the deep satisfaction of pursuing a purpose that his whole understanding recognized as the genuinely ultimate or adequate purpose. Second, the way to serve and glorify God is to promote the creative process, to contribute to the general welfare or common good, in which the man's own future happiness would be included so far as compatible with that of others. Thus the man could retain the natural human sympathy for his own future possibilities, just as he would retain the natural human sympathy for other persons. But all these values, including the joy of serving them, would be viewed as contributory to one achievement, the enrichment of the divine life. For if we enjoy serving God, this our enjoyment of serving him is itself a service, since God, too, is a sympathetic being and delights in our delight. Thus in being utterly devoted, altruistic, in relation to God, we would include all the self-interest that has a right to be included in the ultimate purpose. We should be willing to be damned for the glory of God, but should know that in the very act of so willing, we should, for that moment, enjoy essential salvation.

But only for the moment? Yes, and no. We must remember that the divine omniscience overcomes the seeming fragility of achievement and renders it immortal. Thus each moment of true salvation is a thing of beauty and a joy forever in the divine life. In Whitehead's sublime words, such moments "perish, and yet live forevermore."

Causal Adequacy or Divine Power

Religious faith imputes to God at least the kind and degree of power that the world needs as its supreme ordering influence. Or, more briefly, it imputes power adequate to cosmic need. It comes to the same thing to say that divine power must suffice to enable God to maintain for himself a suitable field of social relations, and thus to maintain himself as a social being. His power is absolute, if that means absolute in adequacy, or such that greater power would be no more adequate, and therefore would not really be "greater"—since adequacy is the measure of greatness, on our theory. What then is adequacy of cosmic power? It is power to do for the cosmos (the field of divine social relationships) all desirable things that could be done and need be done by one universal or cosmic agent. Adequacy is *not* power to do for the cosmos things that could only be done by nonuniversal agents. There are such things, and they are the free acts of localized beings, such as man. For God to do what I do when I decide my own act, determine my own concrete being, is mere nonsense, words without meaning. It is not my act if anyone else decides or performs it. To say, then, that omnipotence is the power to do anything that could be done is to equivocate or talk nonsense. There *could not* be a power to "do anything that could be done." Some things could only be done by local powers; some only by cosmic power. The cosmic status of the latter cannot consist in its ability to "do anything."

What then is this cosmic status? Is it power to get local agents to do anything they could do, power to make or cause them to do it? No, for in spite of what Thomists say, it is impossible that our act should be both free and yet a logical consequence of a divine action which "infallibly" produces its effect. Power to cause someone to perform by his own choice an act precisely defined by the cause is meaningless. The cause can set conditions more or less favorable to such a choice; but if it is a choice, then, in spite of these conditions, the choice is not in all aspects inevitable and may not occur. What would be gained if we did verbally admit that God has caused all events, even free choices, to occur just as they have occurred? We would then face the implication that the most wicked acts are caused by God, made inevitable (even though "not necessary") by his decision. Also, the most unfortunate occurrences and the most bitter suffering and frustrations must be justified as selected by deity for some wise and kindly purpose.

Let us try again. Adequate cosmic power is power to set conditions which are maximally favorable to desirable decisions on the part of local agents. Maximally favorable conditions cannot imply that the most desirable local decisions will be inevitable. For decision is by its very nature not wholly inevitable. To see what maximally favorable, or optimal, conditions would be, we must consider that there are two opposite extremes as to conditions, neither of which would favor desirable decisions. One would be a condition which reduced the degree of local freedom, the range of its alternatives, to a minimum, so that while the resulting local decisions would not be strictly inevitable, that in them which was not inevitable would be so slight as to constitute only negligible danger or risk of evil from the unfortunate use of the freedom. That the risk of evil should thus be reduced to a minimum seems in itself desirable. But we all know that a situation in which practically no harm can be done is not necessarily a very desirable situation. Harmlessness is hardly the *summum bonum*. The question must always be asked, *how much good* can be done in the situation? If the risk or threat is slight, perhaps the opportunity or promise is equally slight. Great opportunity and great risk seem in fact to go together. And this is no mere accident. Great good means great sensitivity and intensity. But great evil arises from the same source, great sensitivity and great intensity. Given beings of slight intensity, slight scope of alternative reactions, the harm they can do each other will be slight; for great suffering, high tragedy, is beyond their natures. But so is great joy, profound happiness. Great value consists in experiences characterized by wide ranges of freedom and capacity for intense sympathetic responses. Given a number of beings thus greatly free and deeply sympathetic, it must be partly chance how far their several decisions harmonize and how far they conflict. An optimum setting of conditions for such freedom will mean neither a degree of safety, mitigation of risk, that would be too dearly paid for in depression of opportunity *nor* a degree of opportunity or promise that would be too dearly paid for in inflation of risk. A too tame and harmless order and a too wild and dangerous, even though perhaps exciting, disorder—these are the evils to be maximally avoided in some golden mean. Observe that the golden mean is not between amounts of evil balanced against amounts of good, but between chance of evil and chance of good, between risk and opportunity, between threat and promise. What actually happens is not some ideal mean determined by cosmic power, some best possible state of the universe. Only the conditions under which the local agents determine local happenings are optimized by deity; the result is not ideal, for the local agents are not optimally wise or good, and cannot be.

The foregoing doctrine demonstrates that the alternative, chance *or* providence, is invalid. Providence is not the prevention of chance, but is its optimization. Chance is just as real as some of the atheists have been telling us during the centuries. But chance is within limits, and these limits cannot be set by chance, for chance limited by chance is the same as chance not limited at all. And chance not limited at all is sheer chaos, everything together, or nothing at all. The reality of chance is the very thing that makes providence significant, as I believe any rigorous development of the cosmological argument will show. As with so many other traditional issues, such as that between absolutism and relativism, so with this one between blind chance and teleology or providence, the solution is, *both*—though not in respect to the same aspect of existence. And no longer do we face the cruel alternative: either no divine control or the deliberate divine contriving of all our woes. The details of events—and our sufferings are among the details —are not contrived, or planned, or divinely decreed. They just happen—period. What is decreed is that it shall be possible for them to happen, but also possible for other, and partly better, things to happen. And the reason their possibility is decreed is that, in view of the state of things, as already determined by past decisions, divine and not divine, no other range of possibilities would involve a more favorable ratio of risk and opportunity. Not that the divine fiat limiting chance is the best possible; for in that case it would be the only possible choice—since the adequate motivation could not choose second best. That is the trap Leibnitz fell into. An only possible act is no act, and no choice. But the divine fiat must be as good as any other possible one. Thus God is free in what he does, and yet is

not free to act in inferior fashion. He is slave to his goodness, if you will. But he can express this goodness as he
pleases in any world arrangement that is not inferior to
any possible other, so far as God determined or might determine it.

Of course I do not claim to have observed as an empirical fact that the ratio of risk and opportunity in the world,
as determined by deity, is as favorable as any possible, in
view of antecedent decisions. Without being omniscient,
how could anyone make such an observation? What I have
done is to formulate an idea of adequate cosmic power that
is apparently free from the absurdities that haunt traditional notions of omnipotence.

It has become customary to say that we must limit divine
power to save human freedom and to avoid making deity
responsible for evil. But to speak of limiting a concept
seems to imply that the concept, without the limitation,
makes sense. The notion of a cosmic power that determines
all decisions fails to make sense. For its decisions could
refer to nothing except themselves. They could result in
no world; for a world must consist of local agents making
their own decisions. Instead of saying that God's power
is limited, suggesting that it is less than some conceivable
power, we should rather say: his power is absolutely maximal, the greatest possible, but even the greatest possible
power is still one power among others, is not the only power.
God can do everything that a God can do, everything that
could be done by "a being with no possible superior."

In another manner of speaking, we may say that deity
is the absolute case of social influence; but even the absolute case of such influence is still—social. This means, it
takes account of the freedom of others, and determines
events only by setting appropriate limits to the self-
determining of others, of the local agents.

That divine power does not wholly determine things may be seen by analyzing more closely what is meant by power. Whatever else God controls, he controls human minds. How then can minds be controlled? There is but one positively conceivable way. A mind is influenced by what it knows, by its objects. He who knows A but not B is different from him who knows B but not A. If God can alter the object of our awareness, he can alter our awareness, alter us. The question then becomes, how can he alter (with supreme efficacy) the object of our awareness? Again, there is but one conceivable way. Suppose he is himself the supreme and indeed the total object that is or can be given to us. (Note, I say, not the sole object, but the total object. The total containing A, B, and C is distinguishable from A or B or C, and therefore the total may be the inclusive object of awareness without being the sole object, since A, B, and C are also objects.) Then to alter us he has only to alter himself. God's unique power over us is his partly self-determined being as our inclusive object of awareness. Thus we return to Plato's self-moved mover of others. Only on that assumption have we the least notion of what "power" in this application is to mean. It is easy to say, "God has power over us." It is another question whether any meaning corresponds to the words. There is meaning if there is meaning to the idea of partial self-determination, and if we can conceive that God, as self-determined, is the essential object of our awareness. Then, as this object changes, we are compelled to change in response.

It also follows that the exact manner of this response cannot possibly be compelled or determined by God. For it is logically impossible that an object should dictate to awareness precisely how it is to respond to the object. A particular awareness of X is something more than just X, and can in no way be necessitated by X. If there were such necessity, there could be but one awareness of a given object, and no two awarenesses could have the same object in common. The doctrine of realism that being known by a particular subject is adventitious to the known means that the exact manner of being known is accidental, too. In any case, there must be an infinity of ways in which beings whose mode of knowing is imperfect or inadequate can respond to an object. There is always a variety of ways of falling short of perfection and, therefore, the object cannot of itself determine the imperfect response.

It may seem, however, that since the divine, which is our object, is omniscient, it must strictly characterize and imply us as we are, including the "response" above spoken of, and so this response cannot fail to be fully determined by the divine knowing. There seem to be at least two ways of dealing with the difficulty. First, if a human experience, E, and the divine knowing of E which is its objective "contemporary" (see Appendix to Chapter II), then the two are "mutually determining," neither preceding the other as premise. Therefore each is partly free in relation to the other. Or, second, E precedes the particular divine state which knows it, and the divine as object of E is not the state in question, but the divine as certain to be expressed by *some* state or other having the abstract character "omniscient of E" (which character, as the Appendix argued, is a universal, not a particular). It is also to be noted that "subject" above does not mean a person, such as God, but a single experience or cognitive state. Being-known-by-God is necessary to all things, in a manner we are about to indicate, but unless the "contemporaneous" conception is valid, this would never refer to any particular cognitive state of deity as necessary to the thing known.

It may be asked how it can be that God constitutes the essential and inclusive object of our awareness. The answer is in some measure easy to see. (Its full explication would amount to the proofs for God's existence.) Only an adequate awareness can fully measure and contain the being and value of everything. We are what the ideal knower knows us to be, our value is that which we have for the ideal valuation, and if we were not thus adequately known and valued, we should have no determinate, objective, public being and value. It is not that we are made what we are simply through being known and valued by deity; as the realists rightly insist, merely being known does not suffice to constitute the existence of anything. The point is, we know we are (or will be) known; our being entirely known is itself known by us. We enjoy God's enjoyment of ourselves. This enjoyment-of-being-enjoyed is the essential factor in all our enjoyment. Nor is this a paradox. We experience every day how much we enjoy being enjoyed by other human beings. Who so happy as the successful singer or actor in the hours of imparting supreme joy to multitudes! How much more is the value of living due to the secret, yet ever-present sense of being given, with all our joy and sorrow, to God! For, other men being also similarly given to God, whatever joy we impart to them we also impart to deity. And only God can adequately enjoy our joy at all times, and forever thereafter through the divine memory, which alone never loses what it has once possessed.

Since an object always influences, but cannot dictate, the awareness of itself, we influence God by our experiences but do not thereby deprive him of freedom in his response to us. This divine response, becoming our object, by the same principle in turn influences us, but here, too, without removing all freedom. The radical difference between God and us implies that our influence upon him is slight, while his influence upon us is predominant. We are an absolutely inessential (but not inconsequential) object for him; he is the essential object for us. Hence God can set *narrow* limits to our freedom; for the more important the object to the subject, the more important is its effect upon the range of possible responses. Thus God can rule the world and order it, setting optimal limits for our free action, by presenting himself as essential object, so characterized as to weight the possibilities of response in the desired respect. This divine method of world control is called "persuasion" by Whitehead and is one of the greatest of all metaphysical discoveries, largely to be credited to Whitehead himself. He, perhaps the first of all, came to the clear realization that it is by molding himself that God molds us, by presenting at each moment a partly new ideal or order of preference which our unself-conscious awareness takes as object, and thus renders influential upon our entire activity. The total or concrete divine mover is self-moved, as Plato correctly said. Only he who changes himself can control the changes in us by inspiring us with novel ideals for novel occasions. We take our cues for this moment by seeing, that is, feeling, what God as of this moment desiderates.

The foregoing account challenges comparison with the traditional view, which merely says that God creates out of nothing, and that his rule of the world is essentially the same as this creation. Scarcely the faintest glimmer of insight from experience seems to shine through such language. Our knowledge that objects influence but do not coerce subjects is left entirely unexploited. Is this the way to attain even the slight comprehension we are capable of— to pay no attention to the one mode of influence we in some degree understand?

Divine Personality

Maximizing relativity as well as absoluteness in God enables us to conceive him as a supreme person. The absolute is neutral between any and all relational alternatives; surely a person cannot be thus neutral. If God be in all aspects absolute, then literally it is "all the same" to him, a matter of utter indifference, whether we do this or do that, whether we live or die, whether we joy or suffer. This is precisely not to be personal in any sense relevant to religion or ethics. But as we have seen, God is not neutral to relationships, except *qua* absolute, and this means, taken merely with respect to the generic and universal form of his relationships abstracting from their specific or individual content.

It is often said that God as personal can only be an appearance or expression of the Absolute. And usually the implication is conveyed that the Absolute is more than God, or that God is a self-limitation or even a "descent" of the Absolute into a lower region. These are somewhat confused notions at best. The Absolute is the formal abstract fixed relational type which any concrete state of God exemplifies, and so, if you like, manifests or expresses. Such a concrete state is God as person caring for the creatures he has created. But the abstract relational form is only the form of adequate or supreme personality as such. Personality is not itself a person, even when it is the divine personality. The form of adequate personality is nonpersonal or absolute, even though no other person exemplifies it and thus it is personal, i.e., individual, to God. It is nevertheless nonpersonal in the sense that it does not think or feel or will. The character of a man does not think or will, the man thinks or wills. The abstract does not act, only the concrete acts or is a person. But it is the divine Person that contains the Absolute, not vice versa. The man contains his character, not the character the man. Moreover, a supreme person must be inclusive of all reality. We find that persons contain relations of knowledge and love to other persons and things, and since relations contain their terms, persons must contain other persons and things. If it seems otherwise, this is because of the inadequacy of human personal relations, which is such that the terms are not conspicuously and clearly contained in their subjects. To transfer to the adequately related subject this apparent externality of terms is the opposite of judicious, however often it has been done in the past and is done now. In God, terms of his knowledge would be absolutely manifest and clear and not at all "outside" the knowledge or the knower.

Another reason given for supposing that God is less than the Absolute is that a person is limited by his acts and choices to this rather than that, whereas the absolute is unlimited or infinite. But again we have equivocation. The infinity of the absolute is the infinity of possibility. The absolute form is neutral to alternatives, therefore limited to none of them, but not because it has something lacking to any one of the alternatives. For since the abstract is in the concrete, any concrete case contains the entire unlimited form. The form is unlimited, not because it has all possible cases in actualized form, but because it has no actual case within it, being the common form of all actuality, and no actuality whatever. Possibility is unlimited because it is not actualized at all. It is everything in the form of possibility, nothing whatever in the form of actuality. God merely as absolute is nonactual; God as personal is at least actual. But not God as absolute nor God as personal nor anything whatever can be actual in all possible ways; for that would be absolute chaos and the same as no actuality. There are the two aspects of existence, possibility and actuality; and the existing power which has both aspects is, in its aspect of unactualized power or possibility, infinite and unlimited, but also completely unactualized, and is in its actuality necessarily limited.

A related argument for supposing God less than the Absolute is that God is good and wise and therefore excludes the predicates bad and foolish, leaving them outside himself. By the same reasoning a house which is large and heavy excludes small and light, which must be outside the house. On the contrary the smallness and lightness of the parts of the house are in the house, and yet the house is not small or light. It is not according to logic to suppose that predicates not applicable directly to a thing as a whole must be outside it. They may be inside it as properties of its constituents.

Of course as absolute God is "simple," has no constituents. But this only shows once more that it is God as relative that is the inclusive conception. As relative, God contains an absolute form of which there are no constituents, and he is, rather than merely contains, a relative actuality of which there are constituents. In this way, God is really all-inclusive, and yet is not wicked or foolish; for these properties are restricted to his included beings, and hence do not apply to him as the including being. If A includes B, but not vice versa, then manifestly A does not have the property of being noninclusive which its constituent B has. Yet both inclusiveness and noninclusiveness are of course included in A, the one as its own property, the other as property of its included relatum B. It is truly amazing how theological discussion has proceeded in discussing such matters, how crude or arbitrary its assumptions have often been.

The not uncommon notion of the "absolute limiting itself" is open to objection. The absolute is by definition indifferent to limits. This neutrality is overcome only in and by a concrete particular act, and such an act is already limited and not absolute. The limited is self-limited, the relative is self-relativized, but the absolute is not limited or relativized, even by itself; for this would be contradiction. The absolute remains unlimited, though inactual or nonconcrete. We may say that God limits himself, but it is God, not the mere absolute form in God, that does so. Furthermore it is misleading to say that even the concrete God "limits himself," if by that is meant that limitation in God is in no way due to anything other than God. Terms qualify and limit their relations. Terms that are self-determining subjects, such as man, with a spark of freedom and creativity in them, are also in part self-limiting, and in choosing their own limits they also choose what the limits of God as knowing them shall be. In deciding to do this, not that, I decide that God shall know me as actually doing this, and not know me as actually doing that. I decide the content of the divine knowledge. To decide less than this is to decide nothing whatever, and is not to decide. For omniscience is the measure of reality, and if it is not affected by our decision, nothing is affected.

From all this nothing perhaps follows as to the extent to which man is capable of good "without grace." There is always a divine element in human decisions, and (while man exists) a human element in the divine decisions, but manifestly the human element is radically inferior and radically dependent. How much good we can do except in loving union with God is not in the least settled by what I have said. Certainly it is meaningless to ask what we could do if God did not help us. He always does help us. The question means, I presume, does God help some more than others, or help more sometimes than at other times, or in this way rather than in that way?

An argument which might be used against our view is this: if the absolute as such is abstract and inactual, is this not a limitation? Yet the absolute, I have said, is unlimited. I reply that limitation is used ambiguously in this argument. To be this rather than that, red (in a certain part) rather than blue, or with knowledge that P is true instead of with knowledge that P is false, is to be "limited" in the first sense. Here it is a question of positive alternatives exclusive of each other. But being inactual is no such positive alternative to being actual. It is rather an element in every actuality, the element of generic form (which as such cannot be actual) common to all the alternatives and neutral to the choice among them. To call such a form limited because as the common form it is not also actual as specific form (the only way anything can be actual) is to use the term in at best a vaguely analogous if not simply equivocal sense. There is no question of choice between the common form and the specific forms. The common form cannot not be, whatever specific forms there may or may not be. Contingency, and all that is subject to success or failure, lies outside the common form. "Limitation" is the measure of such success or failure. In that sense the common form is unlimited. It is no success and no failure because, being an element in any possible achievement, itself is no achievement. If it were alone, it would be a common form common to nothing, a possibility with no actualization, an outline outlining nothing, a relational type where there were no relations and no terms, a class without members, which was yet the only class—in short, nonentity.

Some Practical Applications

What can surrelativistic theism contribute to our contemporary social and political problems? Manifestly this is a subject for a book, not a section. Yet the world crisis seems to demand that the subject at least be touched on. Distinguished students have shown that the decay of civilization is not merely a technological affair, but has religious and philosophical elements of great importance.[1] Man cannot live without ideal aims which relate his endeavor and his suffering and his joy to something more lasting and more unitary than the sum of individual human achievements taken merely at face value. Without such an aim, he falls into cynicism or despair, by which the will to live is indefinitely nullified. The conduct of affairs cannot long remain in the hands of persons thus weakened. History seems so far entirely on the side of the doctrine that when the gods go the half-gods arrive. There is never a vacuum of religious power (Heimann). If human reason seems to discredit known religious forms, what ensues is not a sober rational appraisal of merely human factors accepted as such. What ensues is Lenin worship, party worship, state worship, self-worship, despair, sensuality, or some other vagary. The proper reaction to this apparent fact is not necessarily the advocacy of a "return to religion," meaning by that to a religion whose deficiencies were the very reason why men of the highest integrity and wisdom felt dissatisfied with it, and which is deeply entangled in vested interests. What we need is to make a renewed attempt to worship the objective God, not our forefathers' doctrines about him.

Let us list some of the deficiencies of inherited religions.

Otherworldliness—the flight from the one task we surely face, that of human welfare on earth, to a questionable one, the winning of a heavenly passport.

Power worship—the divorce of the notion of supreme influence from that of supreme sensitivity, in the concepts both of deity and of church and state authority.

1. See E. Heimann, *Freedom and Order: Lessons of the War;* F. S. C. Northrop, *Meeting of East and West;* and the writings of Reinhold Niebuhr.

Asceticism—the failure to genuinely synthesize "physical" and "spiritual" values, as shown above all in the failure of practically all the churches to do justice to the meaning and problems of marriage.

Moralism—the notion that serving God is almost entirely a matter of avoiding theft and adultery and the like, together with dispensing charity, leaving noble-hearted courageous creative action in art, science, and statesmanship as religiously neutral or secondary.

Optimism—the denial that tragedy is fundamental in the nature of existence and God; an example being what one may call the pacifism of magical politics: let us (the pacifists) renounce force and there will be neither war nor any very terrible tyranny.

Obscurantism—the theory that we can best praise God by indulging in contradiction and semantical nonsense.

The confusion of deity and humanity in the theory of infallible revelation.

With the possible exception of the last (which seems sufficiently arbitrary on any metaphysical basis), these defects are all connected with the neglect of divine relativity. A wholly absolute God can provide no lasting good inclusive of human achievement save by the dubious notion of an everlasting prolongation of individual or racial human existence, and even then present human achievement is not intelligibly integrated into the permanent achievement. A wholly absolute God is power divorced from responsiveness or sensitivity; and power which is not responsive is irresponsible and, if held to settle all issues, enslaving. A wholly absolute God can make no use of the physical world or of sensory values, for such a God has no receptivity, nothing analogous to sense perception, as enjoyed, for example, in music or in sexual love. A wholly absolute God derives nothing from the physical or indeed the entire created world; to study that world is to study something that contributes nothing to the actuality of deity; to enrich that world is not to enrich the divine life, which is yet the measure of all value. A wholly absolute God is totally beyond tragedy, and his power operates uninfluenced by human freedom, hence presumably as infallibly determinative of all events, and therefore, it seems, there need be no tragedy. A wholly absolute supreme being is a contradiction in terms, since relativity is as truly good as nonrelativity, each in its proper role, the latter as abstract factor, the former as the principle of concreteness.

Suppose, by a frank recognition of divine relativity, the foregoing defects can be remedied, how does this help us face our appalling difficulties? Who can doubt that these difficulties are due in no small measure to the failure of religion genuinely to synthesize power and sensitivity, or temporal and lasting values, or physical and higher social experiences, or hope and realistic acceptance of the tragic aspect of all existence, actual or possible, or piety and respect for logical integrity, or private morals and public good? These unresolved dualisms have split the world and each man within himself.

One reason why the gulf between us and Russia is so great and stubborn is that we are not able with a good conscience to admit to ourselves the extent to which the Russians are, in some respects, more religious in a good sense than we. The Russian people are taught to live for the community; the impieties of hardhearted individualism, or of racial hatred, are in them (whether or not in their leaders) somewhat better controlled. Science is (at least in some aspects) appreciated. The fundamental lack of freedom is on the other side of the shield. And the political outcasts apparently have scarcely any human rights. The Russians have their forms of impiety, but is there not some truth in what Tillich, Niebuhr, Heimann, and the late Bishop Temple have told us, that the Soviets are Christian heretics rather than pagans? The one thing that needs to be added is, *so are we*. When a world faced dire threat of war and slavery, we said, are we our brothers' keeper? When a world in which we have over a third of the capacity to produce is starving and shivering, we do a bit here and there to rebuild the foreign ruins, while we wonder if we can keep our farmers and miners employed (without troubling to learn any economic wisdom we lacked in 1929). We, the only large prosperous country left, wish we could avoid the primary responsibility for the outcome of the present situation. But it is ours. To evade it will be true, profound impiety. The Russians know this and grimly, cynically perhaps, wait for our default. The question is not primarily what are their intentions? The initiative is largely ours. The question is above all what are our intentions? Shall we repent of our worst follies—such as the superstition that "private enterprise" (somewhat overgrown with monopoly) can of itself control the business cycle (or the opposite one that public ownership is a cure-all)—and take the threat to the world future seriously enough to get such a grip on things that the Russians are forced to respect us? Pacifism will not help; mere military maneuvering and planning will not do the job; what is needed is *leadership in world rebuilding*, including no doubt rearrangement of military matters. A combination of belief that tragedy is not a fancy but always a more or less imminent reality, trust that if we tackle a big job with equally large-minded effort (costing us many billion dollars, with other nations induced to participate proportionally) God will somehow gain advantage from this effort for his inclusive achievements; a healthy tension between respect for the wisdom of others (for example, of the democratic socialists in Europe), remembering that our own wisdom is a feeble and broken light, and loyalty to our own wisdom as the best we have—some such combination, issuing in a program that makes it seem unlikely that any nation can better its position by military adventures as rapidly as by the arts of peace, and unlikely that it will be attacked, some such procedure, may save us from the worst that we have reason to fear. This worst is very terrible. Risk is a cosmic ultimate, but intelligent beings, like God himself, have power to modify the locus of the risk and its relation to opportunity. Great opportunities are also there. If our petty pride could be shattered! If we could really act like grown men, and consciously decide as a nation what a tariff policy is for, for example! Shall we tax ourselves to feed other peoples because we don't wish to trade the food for manufactured goods, all the while promising ourselves we shall cut taxes? Again, shall we cut taxes and weaken our foreign policy accordingly, paying for the economy a little later with catastrophe? There are two or three big issues now which it will be dangerous to muddy up with this or that minor hobby. Shall we exert ourselves to save the world from drifting into a situation in which the only question becomes, who will give the signal for the cataclysm and when? Or shall we go on in our prewar way of halfhearted dabbling in world affairs? The next political campaigns may tell the story. Shall we follow those who distract us from everything save our narrowest self-interest? Or shall we focus on reality, which is the content of the life of deity, not a mere offshoot from deity? There is just one sphere of action, this-world-in-God. Americans have come a good way toward learning to face that world. If they can only come farther, and soon! Those who say, one world, without adding in God, may subconsciously be adding it after all. But those who deny that our task is to build one world are not merely heretics. They are apostates, traitors to the minimal ideal of our culture.

Thus, for example, when we Americans, including apparently millions in our Northern cities, indulge in the shameful superstition or half-conscious lie that the color of a man's skin is *the* clue to his classification as a neighbor, worker, or human being, we not only give our communist critics their most valid talking-point, but we betray our own spiritual heritage. This heritage tells us that man is man, rather than wolf or sheep, because he shares with deity the privilege of participating consciously in the creative process, and of consciously finding his joy in the loving service of others. What has color of skin to do with this! The hundreds of thousands or millions of persons who cannot be housed like human beings, or given work that befits their abilities, because segregation devices in practical effect will that they shall not be, and in logic imply that they need not be, these individuals constitute, according to the doctrine of Whitehead and many of our best modern religious minds, not mere external products of an impassive first cause, but integral members of the all-sensitive passive aspect or "Consequent Nature" of the divine, who suffers in and through all their sufferings. If this is what God is, perhaps it is the word, not the reality, that we have of late been worshipping.

There is another kind of apostasy to be guarded against. In Chapter I we saw how the theological paradoxes were due in part to the worship of power, expressed in the axiom, to be a cause is better than to be an effect. We also saw that this axiom contradicts the essential religious insight into the loving or sensitively responsive nature of God. Now George Orwell has well and tellingly shown how the judgment of intellectuals concerning political matters has repeatedly been warped, to an extent that would be ludicrous were it less tragic and disgusting, by the same "worship of power, which is not fully separable from cowardice." That is to be accepted as good and permanent which is obviously producing the most marked effects and seems itself immune to the action of other causes. While all the world was being passive to the Nazis, many were telling us that it was foolish to point out that the Nazis were blackguards. They were bound to win, and what wins is right, or at least, not wrong, they said. Then when there began to emerge a somewhat similar passivity to the might of Russia, some of the same men began to predict the unlimited triumph of that form of totalitarianism, and to reject any judgment upon the suppression of rights which it involves. Now I do not think it fantastic to see in this abject power worship, tinged with cowardice, the working of somewhat the same elements of human nature that helped to fasten medieval theology upon the human mind for so many centuries. Medieval theology said, "God is good and right because he is active while, in relation to him, all else can be only passive. He makes things and pushes them about exactly as he pleases, for he is the perfect one." That the ultimate power is the power of sensitivity, the power of ideal passivity and relativity, exquisitely proportioned in its responsiveness to other beings as causes, did not dawn on the Church theorists, and it certainly is far from the thoughts of some of our intellectuals.

Pacifism is the almost contrary error of supposing that the ultimate or divine power is the only power to be considered. It is God, not men, who can guide all things (subject to the limits assigned to freedom) by the persuasiveness of his sensitivity. We are radically incapable of such unlimited and universal responsiveness. Moreover, there is a power of brute force, which is going to be wielded by someone, and it had better be retained by the conscientious and intelligent as a last resort against the unscrupulous who would, if not thus restrained, gladly accept it as their monopoly.

But if sensitivity is the ultimate power, how can there be another form of power? The answer is that all power is sensitivity; but there is direct and indirect causal action. God acts on all beings directly, as a man's thought acts on his nervous system, and he is acted upon by all things as a man's thought is acted on by his brain cells. But one man's purpose influences another man, telepathy apart, only by first modifying the man's bodily parts, and thence some factor in the inter-bodily environment of both men, such as sound waves. Now each direct link in this causal chain is interpretable, according to the social theory of reality, as constituted by bonds of sympathy, of "feeling of feeling" (Whitehead), for example, as between a human consciousness and the feelings in various nerve cells. But the final result may be that one man causes another man to be starved to death, without any appreciable feeling of how the other feels about this. Thus "brute power" is an indirect relation, never a direct one. But it is none the less practically efficacious, for good or ill, and has to be reckoned with. The one thing we need not and ought not to do is—to worship it!

Conclusion

John Dewey is somewhat given to lamenting (or seeming to lament) that our philosophical and theological ancestors took the path which they in fact took. I, too, find it difficult not to dream of what might have been. Had men not, over two thousand years ago, fallen down and worshiped their own concept of the wholly absolute or immutable, had they taken instead, as the basis of theologizing, the manifest necessity of divine social relatedness to the world, and had they then sought the supreme excellence of deity in the universality, unfailingness, or unique adequacy, of the divine social relativity or "omnipassivity," they might long ago have found, in this unfailing adequacy, as generic quality in and of every concrete act of divine self-relating, the only absolute of which there is theoretical or practical, religious or philosophical, need, and the only one whose meaningfulness and consistency make it even worth while to ask, Is there evidence or reason for belief in an absolute? Those who honestly reflect upon the question, thus formulated, of the existence of God, will perhaps find that, merely in understanding this question, they have come a long way toward answering it.

Let us summarize our position. The divine attributes are abstract types of social relationship, of which the divine acts are concrete instances or relations. A type of relationship is not qualified or relativized by the relational instances which exemplify it. Such a type is nonrelative, yet related to the relative in the abstract form of "some relative thing or other," relative thing as such; and it can be thus related without loss of independence, because dependence means varying with the variable, while "some relative thing or other," relative thing as such, is invariably real. Or, we may say, dependence consists in relationship to something contingent, but "some contingent thing or other," contingent thing as such, exists not contingently but by necessity. That this accident happens, or that accident happens, is accidental, but that "accidents go on happening," some accidents or other, is not itself accidental but a necessary and immutable truth in which is no shadow of turning. And thus the Absolute is definable in positive relational terms, and without ultimate paradox. Therewith falls the ancient obstacle, first clearly seen, apparently, by Carneades, emphasized by Feuerbach and so many others, to conceiving the supreme reality as the living God, the supreme subject of social relations, yet with an absolute character. This absolute character consists in a unique supereminent type of social relations. The divine compassion is not merely, as Anselm said, something in God, other than compassion, which produces upon us the effects of compassion, but is rather an actual sympathy in God. However, in justice to Anselm, we should point out that the unique excellence of the divine sympathetic states does not itself sympathize, is not itself saddened, is never created and cannot be ended or changed by relation to our weal and woe. And this fixed generic excellence is the one eternal causal factor in all good effects, the contrast to all mutability and uncertainty, the one thing which is without possibility of being, or having ever been, otherwise, and which is free of potency, simply and infallibly real.

This essence, although generic, such that innumerable instances exhibit it, nevertheless characterizes solely the one individual, God, who possesses all these instances, since they are all connected by the uniquely intimate continuity of purpose and memory in the one divine life. Thus the divine is indeed *sui generis* and "not in a class," yet there is an infinite and ever-to-be increased class of previous, already actualized, divine experiences in God at each moment. In this sense God, though not in a class, *is* a class, which is not member of any class of similar classes, and one every member of which enjoys dynamic, and not merely logical, connection with every other member. The divine attributes are the class characters of this unique class, new members of which cannot fail to continue to become forevermore, and old members of which can never fade from the memory of new members, in which is the immortality of all our achievements of experienced quality, in ourselves and all for whom we are concerned, and in every fragment of awareness actualized in time. Thus the least such fragment enriches in its own way and measure all subsequent members of the divine class of experiences, whose receptivity or relativity is as unrivaled as their generic quality is absolute, or neutral to all alternatives.

Index of Names

Index of Subjects